When Kids Ask
Sticky Questions

Dave Veerman
Larry Keefauver
Evan Griffin

David C. Cook Publishing Co. Elgin, Illinois—Weston, Ontario

First Aid for Youth Groups
When Kids Ask Sticky Questions

© 1991 David C. Cook Publishing Co.

Scripture quotations are from the *Holy Bible, New International Version* (NIV), © 1973, 1978, 1984 by the International Bible Society. Used by permission of Zondervan Bible Publishers.

Published by
David C. Cook Publishing Co.
850 N. Grove Ave., Elgin, IL 60120
Cable address: DCCOOK
Illustrations by Bill Duca
Design by Randy Maid
Printed in U.S.A.
ISBN: 1-55513-508-0

When Kids Ask Sticky Questions

ABOUT THE AUTHORS

Dave Veerman has more than 25 years of youth ministry experience, including serving as National Campus Life Director for Youth for Christ. Currently he is vice president of the Livingstone Corporation, a company devoted to helping Christians and Christian organizations improve their ministry effectiveness. Dave is the author of several books on youth ministry, including *Reaching Kids Before High School* and *Youth Evangelism* (SonPower).

Dave wrote the "Answering Sticky Questions without Getting Stuck" article for this book.

Dr. Larry Keefauver is a freelance writer and former youth pastor living in New Smyrna Beach, Florida. He also works with the Youth Ministry Consultation Service, an organization designed to "equip the saints for the task of . . . building up the body of Christ."

Larry wrote sessions 1-10 of this book.

Evan Griffin and his wife Kimberly have discipled high school and college students for several years. They serve with the Navigators at the University of Cincinnati, where Evan also teaches interpersonal communication and public speaking. Evan is the author of the "More Tough Questions" sessions in the Hot Topics Youth Electives series (Cook).

Evan wrote sessions 11-15 of this book.

DOES YOUR GROUP NEED FIRST AID?

Wise is the youth worker who heeds this rule: "Expect the unexpected."

Whether they're as intensely personal as an eating disorder or as far away as a famine . . . whether they're as "minor" as a question about rock music or as devastating as a suicide . . . problems, questions, attitudes, and crises will arise that disrupt the life of your group.

Is it really possible to prepare for such disruptions? Now it is—with "First Aid for Youth Groups."

Each book in the "First Aid for Youth Groups" series is designed to help you respond quickly to specific issues, situations, and events that affect your group.

With the practical, biblical advice contained in each session, you'll be able to help your group members handle and learn from such crises as an accident or natural disaster, a terminal illness, or a teen's pregnancy. You'll be ready to respond to group members' questions as to whether a Christian can be gay or why God could allow good people to go to hell. You'll be prepared to address specific reasons for group apathy or immaturity. And you'll be able to help group members deal with such personal hurts as sexual abuse and physical impairment.

Created with the help of veteran youth workers, these sessions do more than address the problems and crises affecting individuals in your group. They're also designed to raise the sensitivity of other group members, and to cause the group itself to be an instrument of healing.

No one can solve serious problems with a meeting or two. But with "First Aid for Youth Groups," you can be ready with immediate help when symptoms appear. The prescription: Pick sessions as needed and apply the wisdom of God's Word directly to your group.

— **Randy Southern, Series Editor**

ANSWERING STICKY QUESTIONS WITHOUT GETTING STUCK

As Chuck prepared to wrap up the meeting, the members of his group sat quietly, their silence broken only by distant sounds of traffic. *Everything's gone great so far,* thought Chuck. *I've never seen the group this attentive.* He began his closing remarks, using well-chosen words to communicate God's concern for how people live and to motivate his students to moral purity.

"But wait a minute, Chuck," interrupted Matt. "What about gay guys and lesbians? Do they go to hell?"

Now *that's* a sticky question—at a sticky time!

Whether they're ill-timed, public interruptions or carefully worded, private whispers, sticky questions are part of youth ministry. Questions can be sticky because of the *topic* (controversial, personal, or "taboo"), the *timing,* or the *tact* (how they're asked). Whatever the case, youth workers should be prepared "to give an answer . . . with meekness and fear" (I Peter 3:15, KJV).

How Not to Respond

There are wrong ways to respond to sticky questions, and I have seen (and have been guilty of) many of them. Here are four.

1. "What about masturbation?" asks a sophomore girl. Jim, the leader, turns red and mumbles an incomprehensible answer. That's the *embarrassed* response.

2. Then there is the *ignorant* response. This happens when the leader has no idea what to say but pretends to have an answer, uttering a string of hollow words that would do a politician proud.

3. Another approach is *pontification,* The pontificator is sure that he or she has the black-and-white truth about everything. When freshman Chris wants to know about rock music, for example, the leader's dogmatic answer shuts down discussion.

4. Finally, there's the *put-down* response. The questioner is criticized for even thinking, let alone asking, about certain subjects. "Christians don't ask those questions" is the message that comes through loud and clear.

Effective youth workers avoid those types of responses. They attempt to answer each question honestly and responsibly.

Types of Sticky Questions

Before we get into how to respond responsibly, let's look at the sticky questions themselves. The *type* of question will help shape your response.

Sticky questions seem to fall into three categories:

1. intellectual/controversial;
2. emotional/controversial; and
3. very personal.

Regardless of the category, a responsible answer must offer *support to the questioner* and *valid reasons for the response.* But how those two ingredients should be mixed will depend on the type of question and the questioner.

For example, a question in the *intellectual/controversial* category would be:

"What does the Bible teach about capital punishment?" In my three decades of youth ministry, I have never worked with a young person who aspired to be a judge or who had a relative on death row. So whenever this question came up, I could assume it was a purely academic or intellectual one. Capital punishment is controversial in our society, but it's not very personal with most students—and not one they usually get highly emotional about. So the answer should be heavy on the "reasons" side and light on the "support" (unless your questioner actually has a relative or friend who faces execution).

A question about rock music, on the other hand, would fall into the *emotional/controversial* category. It's an intellectual issue, but most kids feel deeply about their music and can get pretty worked up about it. Here the answer should include solid reasons *and* give firm support to the questioner.

An example of a *very personal* question might be abortion. Suppose a girl were to ask whether abortion is wrong. This girl may be considering having an abortion, may have had one, or may have a close friend who is pregnant. In this situation the reasons are important, but the response must be overflowing with support. The leader should honestly share what he or she believes and state why, but he or she must be sensitive to what the person may be going through and communicate affirmation, love, and concern in the style and content of the response.

How to Respond

Now let's consider the steps we can take in answering sticky questions so that we don't get stuck.

Step 1: Take it in stride. Regardless of what is asked, keep your cool and try not to act shocked. This applies to group situations as well as to individual counseling appointments. Even if the questioner is trying to embarrass you or put you on the spot, you will defuse his or her attempt by staying calm and treating the question and questioner with respect. Even a question asked for the wrong reasons can turn out for good. See these questions as opportunities, not threats.

The fact that kids are asking is a *good* sign. It shows they are thinking beyond the surface, that they aren't afraid to say what they (and possibly many others) think. It shows they feel safe in the group, and that they think you can help them find the answer.

Step 2: Affirm the person. Thank the questioner for asking his or her question, even if it's not appropriate. You could say something like: "That's a great question, Heather. I'm afraid it would take too long to discuss it right now, but let's make that our whole topic of discussion next week." Or, "John, I really appreciate your honesty and willingness to say what's on your mind. Most of us have probably wondered about that. Thanks for getting it out into the open."

Don't go overboard with this, but let the person know that it's good to ask questions and that you appreciate the fact that he or she is thinking things through and is looking for answers.

Step 3: Determine the motive. This is a very subjective step, so be careful. What you decide here will often determine how you will frame your answer. Why is the individual asking the question? Is the person sharpshooting, trying to give you a hard time, not really desiring an answer? Is this the real question, or does the questioner have a hidden agenda? Is the individual sincerely looking for truth?

The Bible makes it clear that we should avoid foolish arguments and discussions (Titus 3:9), but it is also a biblical principle that people should seek the truth (Hebrews 11:6). So if someone wants to draw us off onto a tangent or into a meaningless, trivial discussion, we should gracefully avoid it. But we should seriously engage those who are sincere and honest.

If you know the questioner well, you will probably have a good idea about his or her motive. If Todd has a history of making bold statements or asking controversial questions at inappropriate times, his latest query probably falls into that category. If Carin is struggling with her home life and is dealing with a lot of anger, her pointed question about God's justice may not be the real issue—she may have another question beneath the surface.

But if you don't know the student well and there's no previous pattern to refer to, you will have to take the question at face value: as an honest attempt to find an answer.

Step 4: Choose your words carefully. What you say as you begin to answer is very important. With any controversial topic, people have very strong opinions on both sides. So don't alienate half your crowd by jumping quickly to one side of the issue.

I remember a young man who came to our Campus Life meetings. He claimed to be an atheist and was giving some of our kids a hard time about their beliefs. I offered to get together with him after school, and he jumped at the chance. We began our discussion with his explanation of all his reasons for not believing in God. I listened quietly. Then I thanked him for his honesty and explained how I agreed with much of what he had said. In fact, I said, I probably didn't believe in that kind of god either. I could see his defenses melt as we established common ground. Then I was able to explain what I believed God was really like, and we continued our discussion.

One of the best ways to begin is to admit that there are two sides to the issue, even if you firmly believe that one side is almost totally wrong. Take the issue of abortion. I believe that abortion is murder and that it is wrong in just about every imaginable situation. But I also know there are many wonderful, sincere people on the opposite side of the issue. They have some good things to say and some important points to make. It would be a mistake to begin my answer or a discussion on the topic by saying something like, "According to the Bible, an unborn baby is a human being, so abortion is murder."

It would be better to say something like, "This is a very controversial and emotional topic in our society today. One side says that women should have the choice about what to do with their bodies and the fetus growing within them, and that one of the options should be abortion. The other side says that the fetus is a human life, so the mother's choice should not include abortion because that would be murder."

Then I could ask for opinions and begin a lively discussion. Or I could carefully lay out the arguments on both sides and eventually state my convictions.

Choose your opening words with care. And with everything you say, *be fair* and *be honest.* If something is your opinion and not a fact, say so. If you don't know something, admit it. This will encourage your students to be open and honest in their statements, too.

Step 5: Be a guide. Perhaps the easiest way to respond to any question, including a sticky one, is to give an answer and move on. But that wouldn't be the most helpful approach. Remember, we're in ministry—trying to help young people come to faith in Christ and then grow in their faith. In other words, we should help them find the answers themselves, not just accept what we say as Gospel truth.

It's not that we shouldn't have opinions. It's best to have thought through most of the hot issues and to have found our own answers. And it's all right to let kids know what we believe. But we should lay out the facts and the biblical principles, encourage kids to think things through, and then guide them to decide for themselves. This is true even when the issue is clear-cut. Students still should see the truth for themselves, and not just take our word for it.

Step 6: Be a learner. Believe it or not, there will be times when a question may arise for which you do not have an answer. There's so much going on in the world that it's virtually impossible for anyone to be up-to-date on every temptation, conflict, cultural phenomenom, and social aberration. For example, how do you feel about the abortion pill, the crude oil spill, the machine that will kill, the new landfill, the living will, and Capitol Hill? Every evening newscast brings new controversies that could turn into sticky questions.

When you're stumped, don't fake it. Admit that you don't know and that you will try to find an answer. Even if you are well-versed and rehearsed, it's good to let students know that you are open to new information. Be a learner and thus encourage them to continue to seek the truth with you.

Any Questions?

Sticky questions are part of youth ministry. They come with the territory. So don't be surprised when they come to you. As I recall, Jesus Himself was asked quite a few (e.g., "Whose wife will she be in the resurrection?").

Adolescent minds are growing, developing, and gaining perspective—and they want to know. Don't see their questions as threats or insults; regard them as opportunities to help kids think and find the answers for themselves. And if you need information and a way to discuss some of these questions in a group, use this book. That's why it was written. Just remember to take the questions in stride, affirm the person, determine the motive, choose your words carefully, be a guide, and be a learner.

— **Dave Veerman**

Gay Rights activists proclaim that homosexual men and women are discriminated against in our society. These activists have demonstrated in major cities seeking legislation that guarantees all their civil liberties. They contend that one's sexual preference and lifestyle are inalienable rights, and that homosexuality is as normal as heterosexuality. People who disagree with the activists' position are labeled "judgmental" and "prejudiced." Yet the Bible clearly asserts that homosexual activity is sinful, and a violation of God's law.

Is it possible to condemn the sin of homosexual activity while still proclaiming God's love for the sinner? What do we say to those Christians who claim to be followers of Jesus Christ and are gay?

CAN A CHRISTIAN BE GAY?

Specific Aims

• To help kids understand that homosexual activity is a sin; to help kids recognize that a Christian may have homosexual thoughts, but those thoughts need to be turned over to God rather than acted on; to help kids recognize and avoid prejudice toward homosexuals.

Scriptural Support

• Genesis 1:27; 2:20-25; 18:16—19:29
• Matthew 19:4-6
• Romans 1:24-27; 7:14-25
• I Corinthians 7:1-5
• Galatians 6:7
• Ephesians 5:22-32; 6:10-18
• Hebrews 12:4-11
• I John 1:9; 3:9; 4:4

Special Preparation

• Bibles
• Copies of Student Sheet 1-A ("The Truth about Homosexuality")
• Copies of Student Sheet 1-B ("A School Dilemma")
• Pencils
• Chalkboard and chalk or newsprint and marker
• Paper
• Large overcoat
• Hair dryer
• Bowl of water
• One sock
• Coffee cup
• Newspaper

1 FOR WHAT PURPOSE WAS IT CREATED?

To introduce this session, say something like: **Today we're going to be discussing a very controversial subject—homosexuality. I know that over the years you've probably heard—and perhaps even said—some cruel things about homosexuals. The point of our study is not to put anyone down. We know that God's love is for everyone.**

Jesus tells us in the Sermon on the Mount that we are not to condemn people. But we *can* distinguish between what honors God and what He rejects. With that in mind, let's see what God says about homosexuality and how we can respond to homosexual people with both honesty and the good news of God's love.

Put the following objects on a table: a large overcoat, a pencil with an eraser, paper, a hair dryer, a bowl of water, a sock, a coffee cup, and a newspaper.

Say something like: **Everything is created for a certain purpose. However, some objects may be used for purposes other than what they were created for. Tell me what you think the creator of each of these objects had in mind as its correct usage.**

Hold up the coat and ask: **For what purpose was this coat created?**
A. Put the coat on backwards.
B. Put the coat on normally.
C. Put the coat on as if it were a pair of pants.
Ask group members to vote for A, B, or C.

Hold up the pencil and say: **Let's try another object. For what purpose was this pencil created?**
A. To erase.
B. To write.
C. To wear behind one's ear.
Demonstrate each action as you say it. Ask group members to vote for A, B, or C.

Hold up the hair dryer and say: **For what purpose was this hair dryer created?**
A. Put the sock in the water, wring it out, and then start blowing it dry with the hair dryer. **For drying socks.**
B. Hold the hair dryer under the coffee cup. **For heating a cup of coffee.**
C. For drying hair.
Ask group members to vote for A, B, or C.

Hold up the newspaper and say: **For what was this newspaper created?**
A. Making paper airplanes.
B. Reading the news.
C. Cleaning up spilled water.
Ask group members to vote for A, B, or C.

Say something like: **Each of these objects could be used for any of the purposes mentioned, but each object was created with only *one* of the purposes in mind.**

Likewise, for what purpose was sexuality created? To answer that question, we must back up and ask, where did our sexuality come from?

2 SEX: WHERE DID IT COME FROM AND WHAT'S IT FOR?

Have group members form four teams. Assign each team one of the following Scripture passages:

- Genesis 1:27; 2:20-25
- Matthew 19:4-6
- I Corinthians 7:1-5
- Ephesians 5:22-32

Instruct each team to read the assigned passage and determine where sexuality came from and what its purpose is. Give the teams a few minutes to work; then have them share their answers with the rest of the group.

Use the following information as needed to supplement discussion.

Genesis 1:27; 2:20-25—God created man and woman, so He is responsible for designing in us the capacity to enjoy sex; God also directed man and woman—as husband and wife—to become "one flesh."

Matthew 19:4-6—A man and woman become "one flesh" to signify their unity; once they are united, they are not to be separated.

I Corinthians 7:1-5—A man and woman resist sexually tempting situations by fulfilling each other's sexual needs in the marriage relationship.

Ephesians 5:22-32—The intimacy of a marital relationship is symbolic of Christ's relationship to the church.

Distribute copies of Student Sheet 1-A ("The Truth about Homosexuality") and pencils. Have group members answer the true/false statements.

After everyone has answered the questions, ask volunteers to share their responses with the rest of the group. Don't get into an involved discussion here. Explain that you're just trying to get a sense of how group members feel about the subject.

3 HOMOSEXUALITY AND ITS CONSEQUENCES

Point out that one of our modern words for homosexual behavior—sodomy—comes from the name of the ancient town Sodom. For those group members unfamiliar with the biblical account of Sodom and Gomorrah (Genesis 18:16–19:29), explain that Sodom was a town noted for its immorality—particularly its sexual misuse. God punished the wickedness of Sodom by destroying the entire city.

Have volunteers read aloud Romans 1:24-27; Galatians 6:7; and Hebrews 12:4-11.

Ask: **Does God punish homosexual sin today? If so, how?** Point out that God does not rain down fire on sinners today the way He did with Sodom and

Gomorrah. However, we still do "reap what we sow." We will experience the consequences of our sin. Practicing homosexuality can lead to destructive physical and relational consequences which God may use to convict homosexuals of their sin. His discipline is designed to turn people's hearts back to Him. Still, homosexuals do not necessarily suffer in this life because of their sin, any more than others suffer now because of their own wrongdoing.

Have volunteers read aloud I John 1:9; 3:9; 4:4; Ephesians 6:10-18; and Romans 7:14-25.

Ask: **If homosexuals have repented of and stopped their homosexual behavior, but still have homosexual feelings, are they forgiven?** Point out that when we confess our sins—no matter what those sins are—God forgives us. The past is not held against us. But we still live in bodies that are subject to temptation through feelings and thoughts. We have to guard against those temptations. The power of God's Spirit within us can resist any temptation. Feelings and thoughts that tempt us can be overcome through Christ.

If God created us to be heterosexual, why do some people have homosexual desires? Point out that counselors, doctors, psychologists, psychiatrists, and other professionals all seem to have differing opinions on the roots of homosexuality. Some say it's a learned behavior in childhood. Others theorize that some people are born homosexual. God's truth as revealed in Scripture affirms that homosexual activity is a sinful behavior. We have a choice in how we act sexually. The only true knowledge we have about what's right and wrong isn't based on feelings, but on God's Word.

In your discussion of homosexuality, you may want to summarize the following:

(1) Homosexual activity is wrong; being tempted is not (just as is true with other sins).

(2) We're saved by God's free gift of salvation, not because of our works. (If one kind of sin keeps you out of heaven, so would others.)

(3) A person who claims to follow Christ and who rejects the teachings of His Word on the subject of homosexuality is being inconsistent.

4 A School Dilemma

Have group members reassemble into the teams they formed earlier. Distribute copies of Student Sheet 1-B ("A School Dilemma") to each team. Assign two of the teams the "Pro" position and the other two the "Con" position. Instruct each team to follow the directions on the sheet and come up with a list of points it would want to make in the debate regarding the hiring of homosexuals to teach school and the banning of HIV testing.

Give the teams several minutes to prepare. Then have each team present its arguments to the rest of the group. As the arguments are presented, ask a volunteer to write them on the board.

Allow plenty of time for debate and discussion.

5 Taking Action

Distribute paper and pencils to each group member. Ask each person to complete the following:

- **One prayer concern I have regarding this session is . . .**
- **One way I could show compassion to those caught in a homosexual lifestyle is . . .**

Allow a few minutes for group members to think about their responses. If you have time, and if you feel it would be appropriate with your group, have group members form pairs. Instruct them to share what they wrote with their partners and pray about their responses together.

Then close the session in prayer, asking God for His wisdom and strength as your group members attempt to address the issue of homosexuality.

THE TRUTH ABOUT HOMOSEXUALITY

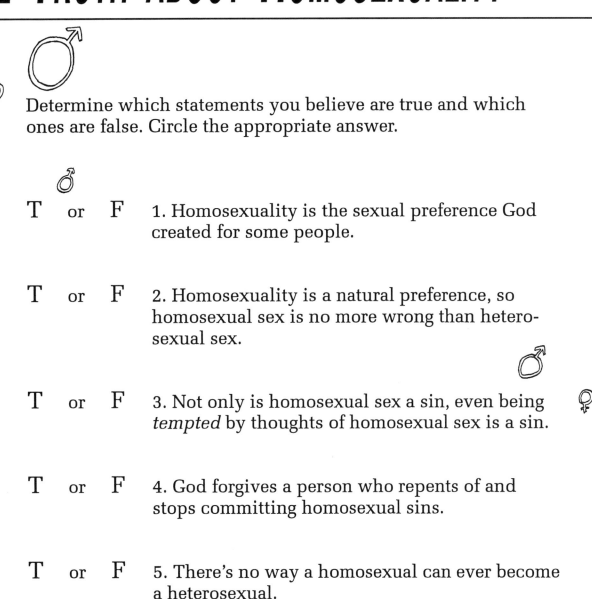

Determine which statements you believe are true and which ones are false. Circle the appropriate answer.

T   or   F   1. Homosexuality is the sexual preference God created for some people.

T   or   F   2. Homosexuality is a natural preference, so homosexual sex is no more wrong than hetero-sexual sex.

T   or   F   3. Not only is homosexual sex a sin, even being *tempted* by thoughts of homosexual sex is a sin.

T   or   F   4. God forgives a person who repents of and stops committing homosexual sins.

T   or   F   5. There's no way a homosexual can ever become a heterosexual.

A School Dilemma

Your group will be debating an upcoming election in your county for an ordinance which affirms the civil rights of people to be hired for all public positions, regardless of their sexual preference. This includes hiring homosexuals for teaching positions in public schools. The law also bans any testing for the HIV (AIDS) virus for hiring people in public positions (including health care jobs).

PRO—You will argue *for* the ordinance, based on the belief that opposing it violates the rights of gays. After all, your side says, sexual preference has nothing to do with a person's qualifications for a job. And if people have to be tested for AIDS before they're hired for a position, shouldn't they have to be tested for other diseases?

CON—You will argue against the ordinance, based on the belief that homosexuality is an unbiblical lifestyle, and that gays should not be put into positions where they could influence the sexual development of young people. And because people with AIDS might infect others, they should be tested before being hired for public positions.

As a group, write a brief summary or a brief list of points you would make for your side of the debate.

Session 2

Very few issues that Christians face are as hotly contested and as potentially divisive as abortion. As you address the topic in your group, it's likely that some heated debate will arise. There's nothing wrong with that. In fact, it should be encouraged.

But in the midst of debate and discussion, don't forget that abortion is an extremely personal subject.

Dave Veerman sums up the personal nature of the abortion issue in his introduction to this book. He writes, "Suppose a girl were to ask whether abortion is wrong. This girl may be considering having an abortion, may have had one, or may have a friend who is pregnant. In this situation the reasons are important, but the response must be overflowing with support. The leader should honestly share what he or she believes and state why, but he or she must be sensitive to what the person may be going through and communicate affirmation, love, and concern in the style and content of the response."

IS ABORTION WRONG?

Specific Aims
• To help group members understand that a "sanctity of life" position seems to correlate with the biblical descriptions of God forming us in the womb (Psalm 139); and to help group members discuss and debate some of the controversial aspects of the pro-life movement—the question of abortion in cases of rape, incest, etc.

Scriptural Support
• Exodus 20:13
• Psalm 51:5; 139:13-16
• Jeremiah 1:4, 5
• Matthew 25:37-40
• James 1:27

Special Preparation
• Bibles
• Copies of Student Sheet 2-A ("My Personal Beliefs")
• Copies of Student Sheet 2-B ("Decide for Yourself")
• Pencils
• Chalkboard and chalk
• Paper
• Newsprint
• Markers
• Index cards

1 FACTS AND FIGURES

Before the session, write the following numbers on the board:

- 25,324
- 498,332
- 116,708
- 407,316
- 54,246
- 58,655

Then prepare six sheets of newsprint and hang them in various locations around the room. At the top of each sheet write the name of one of the following wars: Revolutionary War, Civil War, World War I, World War II, Korean War, Viet Nam War.

Give these instructions: **Each number on the board represents the number of U.S. casualties in a war that the United States has fought. Guess which number goes with which war by writing the numbers on the appropriate sheets. For example, if you thought 54,246 was the number of casualties in the Viet Nam War, you would write that number on the newsprint titled, Viet Nam War.**

When all the group members are finished, review with them the numbers they wrote under each war. Write on the top of the newsprint the number most often appearing under that war.

Then tell the group what the actual casualty numbers are for each war, writing and circling the number at the top of the newsprint for each conflict. The correct answers are as follows:

- Revolutionary War—25,324
- Civil War—498,332
- World War I—116,708
- World War II—407,316
- Korean War—54,246
- Viet Nam War—58,655

Say something like: **You may not have guessed it from our opening activity, but today we will be discussing abortion. Abortion is a complex issue with many perspectives. Some people are personally opposed to abortion but feel that government should not legislate whether or not a woman can have an abortion. Others believe that all abortions are murder. Some say that abortion is wrong except in cases of incest, rape, or threat to the mother's life. Still others insist that abortion is a woman's private choice.**

Not all Christians agree on a single position. All of the positions I just mentioned are loosely categorized under two opposing groups. The first is pro-life, which is essentially against abortion. The second is pro-choice, which advocates leaving the choice for or against abortion solely up to the woman. We will attempt today to explore both positions.

Refer back to the sheets of newsprint hanging around the room. Ask volunteers to guess how the number of abortions performed since the Row vs. Wade decision in 1973 compares to the numbers of war casualties posted. Ask: **Which war's casualty numbers would you guess is closest to the number of total abor-**

tions performed between 1973 and 1990? Allow several group members to respond.

Then explain that 1,160,581 soldiers were killed during all the major wars fought in our country's history. Yet, that's less than the number of abortions performed in the U.S. *each year*. Allow a moment for that statistic to sink in.

Then ask: **Are you surprised to learn that so many abortions are performed each year? Why or why not?** Allow time for response.

Say something like: **Some have called abortion the "Silent Holocaust." In World War II, thousands of innocent Jews were put to death in prison camps throughout Germany. It was called "The Holocaust." Referring to abortion as the "Silent Holocaust" indicates that millions of unborn children who cannot speak for themselves are destroyed.**

How do you feel about calling abortion the "Silent Holocaust"? Do you think it's too strong a term? Why or why not? Allow plenty of time for response.

2 MY PERSONAL BELIEFS

Distribute copies of Student Sheet 2-A ("My Personal Beliefs"). Instruct group members to form small groups of four to complete the sheet. Try to have an equal number of males and females in each group, if possible.

After everyone has had about five minutes to fill out the sheet, ask the members of the small groups to share among themselves their answers to the questions. If possible, try to have each group member share his or her response to each question. However, if a person feels uncomfortable with sharing, he or she may pass.

3 WHAT DOES THE BIBLE SAY?

Explain that the primary area of disagreement on the abortion issue is when the fetus becomes a human being. Those who say that life doesn't begin until birth see abortion as nothing more than the removal of unwanted tissue. Those who say that life begins at conception tend to see abortion as murder.

Instruct each small group to look up the following Scripture passages: Psalm 51:5; Psalm 139:13-16; and Jeremiah 1:4, 5. Say something like: **After reading each passage, try to reach a consensus as a group on what the passage says about whether life begins at birth or at conception.** Allow kids to disagree within these groups.

Give the groups a few minutes to work. Then have each group report its findings. You may want to write the references on the board and then write the groups' responses next to the references.

In discussing the passages, emphasize that phrases like "sinful from the time my mother conceived me," "Your eyes saw my unformed body," and "Before I formed you in the womb I knew you" seem to indicate that life begins at conception.

Read Exodus 20:13 to the group. Instruct each small group to come up with a definition for "murder." Again allow kids to disagree within the groups.

After a few minutes, have the groups share their definitions. Write the definitions on the board as they are given.

Then ask: **Do you believe that abortion fits your group's definition of murder? Why or why not?** Encourage volunteers from each group to respond.

4 DELVING INTO THE TOUGHER ISSUES

Say something like: **The following are some of the arguments used by pro-choice proponents to defend their beliefs. How would you respond to them?**

1. Abortion lessens the number of unwanted children from teenage pregnancies.

2. Families in Third World countries can't afford unwanted children. If they were born, these children would lack food, medicine, and shelter.

3. Abortion keeps children from being born into verbally, sexually, or physically abusive situations.

As your group members offer their responses, read aloud James 1:27 and Matthew 25:37-40 to supplement the discussion.

Ask: **What is our responsibility as Christians to babies born who are unwanted?** (Take care of them.)

If Christians around the world really fulfilled their responsibilities to orphans, the poor, and the unwanted, how might that affect the number of abortions performed each year? (If the mothers of "unwanted" babies had some kind of assurance that their children would be cared for, they might be more inclined to give birth to the kids. Cutting the number of "unwanted" babies aborted each year would make a serious impact.)

Is it realistic for Christians to take on something as universal as caring for unwanted babies? Why or why not? (It's not a matter of *one* person trying to make a global impact; if each Christian worked within his or her means to support an unwanted child, we could *corporately* impact the world.)

5 IF IT AFFECTED SOMEONE YOU KNOW

Distribute copies of Student Sheet 2-B ("Decide for Yourself"). Assign one of the roleplays to each small group. Allow a few minutes for the groups to "choose their options" and prepare. Then have each group perform its roleplay.

After each roleplay, ask the rest of the group: **Would you have chosen that option if you had roleplayed the situation? Why or why not?**

Is that a realistic solution? Why or why not?

Is it possible for people who aren't Christians to reach that conclusion? Why or why not?

After all the roleplays have been completed, ask the members of each small group to determine among themselves what they believe would be the *best* Christian response to their situation. It may or may not be one of the responses on their list. After a few minutes, have each small group share its decision with the rest of the group.

6 PRAYER! COMMITMENT! ACTION!

Give your group members an opportunity to make a commitment concerning the abortion issue. Give each person an index card and a pencil. Read the following list of options slowly a couple of times. Instruct group members to consider the list carefully and determine what he or she would be willing to do. Have group members write their commitments on their cards.

- **Pray daily about abortion issues and the various people involved.**
- **With a few other members of the group, lead an adult group in the church through this session.**
- **Volunteer to be a peer counselor at school.**
- **Determine what you would tell a friend about abortion if asked.**
- **Participate in a rally promoting your position on abortion.**
- **Volunteer to work in a home for unwed mothers.**
- **Volunteer to work in a community agency for preventing child abuse.**
- **Volunteer to work in a community agency for counseling teenage mothers.**
- **Volunteer to work in a hospital nursery, holding and rocking unwanted babies.**

If group members have other commitments they'd like to make that aren't included in this list, encourage them to do so.

Ask group members to bow their heads. Lead them in prayer for the following people:

- mothers and fathers with an unwanted pregnancy;
- mothers and fathers living with the guilt of already having had an abortion;
- legislators faced with having to pass laws about abortion;
- judges rendering decisions in abortion cases;
- pastors and counselors giving guidance to people making decisions about abortion;
- missionaries and Christian workers in Third World countries caring for poor and orphaned children;
- nurses and doctors involved in caring for mothers who have aborted unwanted children.

Also pray for God's strength and leading as group members prepare to make a difference in the abortion issue.

If possible, meet individually with your group members in the coming week to talk about their commitments and to offer your encouragement.

My Personal Beliefs

1. How did you feel when you learned that the number of abortions performed *each year* is greater than the number of U.S. casualties in *all* of America's wars put together? (Circle all that apply.)

Numb   Surprised   Angry   Upset   Unbelieving

Grieved   Sickened   Sad   Confused   Indifferent

2. Which term would you use to describe abortion?

Medical procedure   Fetal interruption

Pregnancy termination   Murder

Genocide

3. When do you think life begins?

At conception

When a baby can live outside the womb

At birth

Silent Holocaust?

4. I believe abortion is . . . (check one)

_____ A woman's choice.

_____ Wrong in all circumstances.

_____ Wrong except when conception occurs due to incest or rape.

_____ Acceptable only if a mother's life is threatened.

_____ Acceptable only if doctors discover that the unborn child is deformed.

DECIDE FOR YOURSELF

BACKGROUND

John and Jean have been dating for months and are sexually active. Both are Christians. Jean discovers that she is pregnant.

SITUATION #1

John shares with some of his best friends that Jean is pregnant. He asks them what they think he should do. Roleplay one of these three scenarios:
- The friends offer to raise the money for an abortion.
- The friends offer to go with John to the pastor for counseling.
- The friends offer to go with John to talk to his parents.

SITUATION #2

John and Jean discuss what they will do. Choose one of the following scenarios to roleplay:
- John tells Jean that some of his friends are willing to raise the money for her to have an abortion.
- John tells Jean the pregnancy is *her* problem, not his.
- John offers to marry Jean and raise the baby with her.
- John suggests that Jean have the baby and give it up for adoption.
- Jean tells John she wants to have the baby and raise it herself without getting married.

SITUATION #3

John and Jean go to one of their best friends and ask for advice. Roleplay one of the following scenarios:
- The best friend offers to go with John and Jean to talk to a counselor.
- The best friend tells them to do whatever they feel is right.
- The best friend tells them that abortion is wrong and that the only decent thing to do is have the baby and get married.
- The best friend suggests that they go and talk with their parents.

SITUATION #4

John and Jean decided on their own that Jean should have an abortion. Afterward, they go to one of their best friends feeling guilty. Roleplay one of the following scenarios:
- The best friend tells them to go to their parents and pastor and confess what they have done.
- The best friend prays with them, seeking the Lord's forgiveness.
- The best friend responds, "Hey, it was your decision. I don't really want to get involved in it."

With the amazing advances of medical science and recent exploration into the mysterious realm of life-prolongation, clashes between science and religion are inevitable. How far is too far? When does science cease to be beneficial and begin to tread in areas where people were not meant to tread? These are some of the questions surrounding the issue of euthanasia.

With the possible exception of abortion, no medical-spiritual issue is as highly publicized and hotly contested as euthanasia, or "mercy killing."

As Christians, we must ask ourselves some questions. Is euthanasia really God's kind of mercy? Is it a dignified way to help people avoid the pain of terminal illness? Or is it merely a euphemism for murder or suicide?

SHOULDN'T PEOPLE BE ALLOWED TO DIE WITH DIGNITY?

Specific Aims

• To help young people understand two arguments of the euthanasia issue: (1) God has given us the medical knowledge to preserve life, so that knowledge should be used to its full extent; and (2) death in some cases may be God's relief given to His suffering children, and should not be interfered with.

Scriptural Support

• Romans 6:23; 8:18-27
• I Corinthians 15:12-19, 50-57
• James 1:17

Special Preparation

• Bibles
• Copies of Student Sheet 3-A ("The Cause of Death")
• Copies of Student Sheet 3-B ("The Sue Adams Story")
• Pencils
• Chalkboard and chalk or newsprint and marker
• Small prizes (optional)

1 LIFESPANS

Open the session with a quiz. Read aloud the following list of living things and have group members guess the average lifespan of each. You may want to award a small prize to the person whose guess is closest each time.

- **Coyote** (21 years, 10 months)
- **American badger** (23 years, 8 months)
- **Dwarf apple tree** (25 years)
- **Yugoslavian men** (64.3 years)
- **White fir tree** (262 years)
- **Worker honeybee born in midsummer** (28 days)
- **Horse** (47 years)
- **Tiger** (26 years, 3 months)
- **American women** (75.2 years)
- **Redwood tree** (1,100 years)

Explain that there is an average lifespan for every living creature. Then point out that, in this session, you're going to be talking about a subject related to the *human* lifespan.

2 POINTS TO PONDER

Say something like: **Today we're going to be talking about euthanasia, also known as "mercy killing" or "death with dignity." Euthanasia can refer to a number of different situations. It may refer to the practice of allowing someone who is in a coma, with no hope for recovery, to die. This is also known as "pulling the plug"—not keeping the person alive through extensive use of medical equipment and drugs.**

Other, more extreme, examples of euthanasia involve allowing a person with a terminal illness to commit suicide before the disease takes its toll.

In this session we'll look at some of the various forms of euthanasia and apply God's word to the decisions surrounding the topic. But before we do that, let's look first at *why* we die.

Read aloud Romans 6:23.

Then say something like: **The wages of sin is death. And since all of us have sinned, we are all destined to die. In Scripture, there are two reasons given for death. The first reason is that death is the natural end to life when the body succumbs to age, disease, violence, or accident—all of which exist because of our state of sin. The second reason is that God sometimes judges people for wicked acts and takes their lives.**

Distribute copies of Student Sheet 3-A ("The Cause of Death") and pencils. Have group members form teams of four. Instruct the teams to read the passages and determine whether the people died naturally or if God took their lives. Give the teams several minutes to complete the sheet.

When everyone is finished, ask volunteers from each team to share their conclusions.

The question of how to categorize Jesus' death will probably come up. If so, try to avoid extensive discussion about it now. Tell group members that you will address it later in the session.

Say something like: **We've seen that, in the Bible, there are quite a few examples of God taking someone's life as the result of sin. Do you think God still takes people's lives today because of their sin? Why or why not?** After several volunteers have shared their opinions, explain that you're not really looking for "correct" answers here; you're just looking for group members' opinions.

Read aloud James 1:17.

Ask: **Would you consider knowledge, particularly medical knowledge, a gift from God?** (Most group members will probably agree that knowledge *is* a gift from God.)

If God has given us the medical knowledge to be able to help someone live longer, is it wrong not to use that knowledge? In other words, are we wasting our God-given abilities if we don't do everything possible to prolong a person's life? Why or why not? Again, explain that you're not necessarily looking for "right" answers; you're just looking for group members' opinions.

Remind group members of the biblical examples of God taking people's lives because of their sin. Then ask: **Is it possible that, in our efforts to prolong a person's life, we might be interfering with God's will for the person?** Allow time for a few volunteers to respond.

3 DECIDING WHEN TO DIE

Say something like: **Because of medical advances, we are now able to prolong life through machines and medicine. In fact, we are now able to sustain life for so long that medical professionals and/or family members may have to decide when to allow a person to die.**

On another front, recent technology has introduced options which allow people to make their own decisions about when they die. Probably the most famous example of this is the controversial "suicide machine."

As Christians, how should we feel about these issues? How much should we do to keep someone alive? How much freedom should we allow someone who wants to die? Let's look at two very difficult situations.

Read the following story aloud.

Eric was a college freshman in Fort Worth, Texas. In a tragic car wreck, his neck was broken. He was paralyzed from the neck down. In order to stay alive, he had to breathe with the help of a respirator. He was fed with a tube. In fact, every function of Eric's body was done with the help of other persons or by a machine.

Though Eric was kept comfortable, the doctors said he was destined to remain paralyzed for the rest of his life. Confined to a bed, he would have to be cared for 24 hours a day. However, he was mentally alert and aware of all that was happening to him.

After much prayer and discussion with doctors, ministers, and family, Eric

asked that he be taken off life-support systems and allowed to die. His doctors honored his request. Two days after the equipment was removed, he died.

Discuss the story, using the following questions.

Would you have made the same decision as Eric? Why or why not?

Do you believe that the family should have kept Eric alive regardless of his decision?

Did they murder him by turning off the equipment?

If you had been a Christian friend of the family, what would you have advised them to do, based on your Christian beliefs?

Encourage several group members to offer their opinions. The discussion may trigger some debate among your group members. If so, allow it to flourish.

Then ask: **Where would you draw the line? Do you believe that we should use medicine to do everything possible to keep a person alive for as long as possible?**

Let's imagine that there's a line across the room. The wall on my left represents the opinion, "Do everything medically possible as long as there's any hope for life." The middle of the room represents the opinion, "If a person is brain dead or hopelessly deteriorating physically—like Eric—then Christian love and mercy would mean pulling the plug." The wall on my right represents the opinion, "If a person is terminally ill, then euthanasia is acceptable." Move to the place in the room that most fits your beliefs.

After everyone has found his or her place, ask volunteers to explain why they chose the spot they did.

Then reassemble the group and read the following story aloud. (Point out that this is based on a true story, but the person's name has been changed.)

Sue wanted to die with dignity. The 54-year-old mother learned that she was in the early stages of Alzheimer's disease, which eventually causes its victims to lose all of their mental capabilities.

Sue knew what was in store for her, and it was too much for her to accept. So even though the disease had not yet begun to seriously affect her thought processes, she made arrangements to end her life.

Sue contacted a retired physician who was willing to help her die. He converted the inside of a rusty van into a "suicide chamber" and rigged up a machine that would allow Sue to send a lethal dose of drugs into her system when she was ready.

After saying good-bye to her family, Sue went through with her plan. Inside the van, hooked up intravenously to the suicide machine, Sue pushed a red button at the base of the machine that triggered a deadly stream of potassium chloride through the tube in her arm. In a few minutes, she was dead.

The doctor said she died peacefully.

Distribute copies of Student Sheet 3-B ("The Sue Adams Story"). Give group members a few minutes to complete the sheet. Then ask volunteers to share their responses.

4 BIBLICAL COMFORT

Have your group members form two teams. Assign I Corinthians 15:12-19, 50-57 to one team and Romans 8:18-27 to the other team. Instruct the teams to look up their passages and determine how those passages could provide comfort to someone who is terminally ill.

Give group members several minutes to work. When they're finished, have a volunteer from each team report on the team's conclusions.

Use the following information to supplement your discussion of the passages.

I Corinthians 15:12-19, 50-57—Death for the Christian is merely the beginning. As surely as Christ rose from the dead, so will we be raised when we die. People who believe this world is all there is are to be pitied because they fail to recognize the eternal aspect of faith in Christ.

Not only will we be raised after our deaths, we will be raised into new, glorious bodies. The ravages of disease and age will no longer affect us in our heavenly forms. So our physical deaths should not be dreaded. Death holds no "sting" for a Christian. But it can be painful and scary and cause our loved ones grief.

Romans 8:18-27—The eternal glory that awaits Christians in the next life will more than make up for the pain and suffering we experience in this life.

Sum up your discussion of euthanasia with the following points:

(1) Most Christians agree that taking your own life is wrong, even to avoid pain or to avoid an "undignified" death later.

(2) Most Christians agree that taking another person's life to keep him or her from suffering ("mercy killing," as with lethal injection) is wrong.

(3) Many Christians would say, however, that artificially extending the life of a brain-dead person is not necessary unless the family, doctor, or legal authority requests it. Many would also say that using "heroic" (unusual, expensive, or experimental) or painful means to prolong the life of a person who is in the final stages of a terminal disease is not necessary unless the person requests it.

(4) Many Christians might allow a person described in (3) to die naturally if the person desires by not forcing the person to take medicine or be hooked up to machines—but would not withhold food or water.

(5) Most Christians do not believe that a poor "quality of life" (being paralyzed, for example) justifies the ending of that life.

5 ONE WHO DIED WITH DIGNITY

Have group members look again at Student Sheet 3-A. Ask: **Which person's death was hardest to categorize?** (Most group members will probably agree that Jesus' death was hardest to categorize, since it fits neither category.)

Say something like: **Jesus died for a reason different from any other. He died** innocently. He died without sin. He laid down His life voluntarily—to save us from our sins. He truly died with dignity.

Say something like: **Because Jesus died for our sins, if we believe in Him, we have no need to fear death—no matter what the circumstances.**

Close the session in an "echo prayer." Read the following statements and have your group members repeat them after you.

I am never alone.

I trust Jesus.

Even though I walk through the valley of the shadow of death.

He is with me.

I fear no evil.

Jesus has died for me.

I will live forever with Him. Amen.

THE CAUSE OF DEATH

Read the following passages, concerning the deaths of famous Bible people. Decide which deaths were due to "natural causes" and which deaths were the result of God's judgment on the person's wickedness or disobedience. Put a check under the column you choose.

PEOPLE	DIED A NATURAL DEATH	GOD TOOK THEIR LIVES
1. Ananias and Sapphira Acts 5:1-11		
2. The people of Sodom and Gomorrah Genesis 19:1-29		
3. Abraham Genesis 25:7-11		
4. Moses Numbers 20:9-13; Deuteronomy 34:1-8		
5. Nabal I Samuel 25:36-38		
6. The Rich Fool Luke 12:13-21		
7. Jesus Luke 23:44-49		

The Sue Adams Story

Put an "X" on the line to indicate your feelings and beliefs.

1. Mrs. Adams' decision to die was:

_____

Merciful to   Not sure   Suicide
herself and
her family

2. The doctor's decision to provide Mrs. Adams with poison was:

_____

A doctor simply   Not sure   Murder
helping a patient

3. If you had been Sue Adams, what would you have done? (Check as many as you feel are appropriate.)

_____Done as she did.

_____Prayed about it.

_____Asked for God's healing.

_____Read the Bible.

_____Asked for medicine to relieve the pain.

_____Asked other Christians to pray for me and counsel me.

_____Done exactly what my doctor advised me to do.

_____Not told anyone about the disease.

_____Other: _____

When was the last time you watched the evening news without hearing of some violent crime that had been committed in your area? Murder, rape, abuse, muggings, and assaults occur so frequently that we become numb to their impact on our total society.

In the U.S. there are over 1,800 violent crimes committed each year per every 100,000 people. A significant proportion of these violent acts are perpetrated by repeat offenders. Some parolees who have murdered, murder again; some who have raped, rape again. And so the violence continues.

Does capital punishment offer both justice and deterrence for violent crimes? What guidelines does the Bible give?

WHAT ABOUT CAPITAL PUNISHMENT?

Specific Aim
• To help young people decide for themselves whether capital punishment is justifiable, "eye for an eye" retribution, or a contradiction to Christ's teachings on forgiveness and loving our enemies.

Scriptural Support
• Genesis 9:6
• Exodus 21:15-17, 22-25, 28-30; 22:18
• Leviticus 20:10-16; 24:10-16, 23
• Deuteronomy 13:1-11; 17:12; 21:18-21; 22:13-21, 25-29
• John 7:53–8:11
• II Peter 3:9

Special Preparation
• Bibles
• Copies of Student Sheet 4-A ("Judge and Jury")
• Copies of Student Sheet 4-B ("Justice and Mercy")
• Pencils
• Chalkboard and chalk or newsprint and marker
• Index cards with references written on them as instructed in the "Capital Punishment: Then and Now" section

1 JUDGE AND JURY

Distibute copies of Student Sheet 4-A ("Judge and Jury"). Have group members form four teams. Assign each team one of the crime stories on the sheet. Instruct the teams to read their stories and discuss them thoroughly. Then have each team decide, based on the facts presented in the story, whether or not the criminal(s) deserves the death penalty. (You may want to explain that, in real criminal cases, manslaughter is not punishable by death.)

Each team should act as judge and jury, deliberating carefully before reaching a verdict. Allow several minutes for the teams to work.

When all the verdicts are in, have each team appoint a "jury foreman." The foreman will read his or her team's crime story to the rest of the group. But before he or she reveals the team's verdict, give the rest of the group an opportunity to guess what the verdict is. When everyone has had a chance to guess, have the jury foreman reveal his or her team's verdict and explain how the team reached that verdict.

After all the teams have had an opportunity to explain their verdicts, discuss the activity using the following questions:

How did you feel about the person(s) who committed the crime? Why?

How did you feel about the victim(s)?

Would your attitude be any different if you were actually part of the jury that convicted the person on trial? In other words, if you knew that your vote could actually cause a person to be put to death, would you change your mind about the death penalty? Why or why not?

Do you believe that the Bible supports capital punishment?

Allow time for several volunteers to respond to these questions.

2 CAPITAL PUNISHMENT: THEN AND NOW

Write the following list on the board:
- Murder
- Manslaughter
- Rape
- Robbery
- Aggravated assault (an assault combined with an intent to commit a crime)
- Kidnapping
- Espionage (spying)

Ask group members to vote on which offenses they believe deserve the death penalty. Discuss why group members chose the ones they did.

Point out that, in the Old Testament, several different crimes were punishable by death. Distribute to several volunteers 3 x 5 cards on which you have written the following references. (You'll probably need to assign three or four cards to each volunteer.)

- Exodus 21:15
- Exodus 21:16
- Exodus 21:17
- Exodus 21:22-25
- Exodus 21:28-30
- Exodus 22:18
- Leviticus 20:10
- Leviticus 20:11, 12
- Leviticus 20:13
- Leviticus 20:14
- Leviticus 20:15, 16
- Leviticus 24:10-16, 23
- Deuteronomy 13:1-11
- Deuteronomy 17:12
- Deuteronomy 21:18-21
- Deuteronomy 22:13-21
- Deuteronomy 22:25-29

Instruct the volunteers to look up their assigned passages, discover what offenses are being described, and then write those offenses on the board.

Ask: **How many of these offenses are still punishable by death today in our society?** (Very few, if any, of them.)

Do you think any of them *should* be punishable by death today? Which ones? Why? Allow several volunteers to offer their opinions.

Then say something like: **Christian believers have differed sharply on the issue of capital punishment.** Read Genesis 9:6 aloud. Say: **Some people believe that this Old Testament command still requires society to put to death anyone found guilty of "shedding another person's blood."**

Other people believe that the Bible's teachings on forgiveness should apply to criminals guilty of violent crimes. Read aloud John 7:53–8:11.

Ask: **Which viewpoint do you hold to? Do you think the Bible requires the death penalty for certain offenses? Or do you think that Jesus' teachings on forgiveness apply to violent crimes?** Encourage several group members to respond. Don't try to reach a "conclusion" here. Just encourage group members to share their opinions.

3 TAKING SIDES

Say something like: **We are now going into a courtroom to hear the final arguments between the prosecution and the defense attorneys in the case of the satanic cult sacrifices.**

Read the description of the case again from Student Sheet 4-A. Then distribute copies of Student Sheet 4-B ("Justice and Mercy").

Divide the group into three sections: prosecution, defense, and jury. Instruct the prosecution to come up with a list of reasons why the death penalty is in order for this case and to write those reasons in the column labeled "Justice."

Instruct the defense to come up with a list of reasons why the death penalty is *not* in order for this case and to write those reasons in the column labeled "Mercy." Give the prosecution and defense several minutes to come up with their lists. When they are finished, have them present their lists to the jury.

Give these instructions to the jury: **As both sides present their arguments, listen for points that make sense to you. If you agree with a point made by the prosecution, write it down in the column labeled "Justice." If you agree with a point made by the defense, write it in the column labeled "Mercy."**

After both sides present their arguments, determine which column outweighs the other. If the arguments for "Justice" are stronger, then you must decide for capital punishment. If the arguments for "Mercy" are stronger, then you must vote for a prison sentence. The way you vote should be determined solely by which column has the longest list of valid arguments.

If you as a jury are not unanimously *for* capital punishment, then you must decide on the length of the prison sentence.

Give the jury several minutes to work. Then have a spokesperson for the jury announce the verdict and explain why the jury reached that conclusion.

Use the following questions to supplement your discussion of the activity:

How did you members of the prosecution feel about seeking the death penalty for the defendant?

How did you members of the defense feel about seeking mercy for the defendant?

How did you jury members feel about your verdict?

How do you think the family members of the victims will respond to the verdict?

Encourage several group members to respond to the questions. Then say something like: **In real life crime stories, there are many things to consider. Not only does a jury hold the criminal's life in its hands, it must also consider the *victims* of the crime—both those dead and those surviving. Will *they* receive justice and mercy along with the criminal? For example, if an innocent person is murdered, why should the murderer be allowed to live? The murderer pronounced a death sentence on the victim and became executioner. Can society permit that murderer to live?** Allow time for brief response.

Then say something like: **In God's covenant with Noah, the death penalty was established. In God's covenant through Moses, murder and several other offenses were to be punished by death. The principle of retribution was also set forth—"an eye for an eye, a tooth for a tooth."**

Jesus takes this concept to a new level of understanding. He suggests that we *love* our enemies and do good to those who have done wrong to us. So, where is the balance between justice and mercy? How do grace (undeserved favor) and forgiveness apply to capital punishment? Allow time for a few volunteers to offer their opinions.

Then say something like: **While the weight of some Scripture seems to tip the scales of justice and mercy toward capital punishment, there is also biblical support for forgiveness and grace. Today we've briefly explored both sides of the issue.**

Some day you may face the issue more realistically when you serve on a

jury or have to vote on the issue. Before you make a decision, seek the leading of God's Spirit through prayer, Bible study, and the opinions of Christians whose judgment you trust.

4 ETERNAL CAPITAL PUNISHMENT

Say something like: **For people who don't know Christ, there is an eternal form of capital punishment. All of us have sinned—and the sentence for being found guilty of sin is death and eternal punishment in hell. Yet God judged our sin and paid the penalty for us through the death of Jesus, His only Son.**

So instead of facing eternal capital punishment, through faith in Jesus, we will know mercy and grace. In mercy, we do not receive the penalty we deserve—eternal punishment. In grace, we receive what we don't deserve—eternal life.

Read aloud II Peter 3:9. Point out that God desires every person, regardless of his or her crimes, to "come to repentance." Close the session in prayer, asking that criminals on "Death Row" may experience Jesus' mercy and grace and escape *eternal* capital punishment.

Judge and Jury

Story 1: College Campus Serial Killer

In Gainesville, Florida, a killer stalked college students. A week before the fall semester was scheduled to begin, several students were found brutally murdered. When the police finally arrested a suspect, he confessed to seven slayings. Without remorse, he gave no reason for the homicides. You are the judge rendering a sentence. What sentence do you pronounce?

Story 2: A Cult Sacrifice

In a town near the Texas-Mexico border, a small group of Satan worshipers lured unsuspecting young people to their remote ranch. There they forced the victims to participate in satanic rituals and ceremonies. During the rituals, the satanists sacrificed the victims to the devil. All of the cult members were eventually caught and found guilty of murder. You are the judge in the case. What sentence do you render?

Story 3: An Abused Child

In South Florida, a mother and father punished their two-year-old daughter by locking her in a closet for days. She was deprived of food and water when she cried. When the young girl upset her parents, she was spanked until she was black and blue.

During one of the punishment sessions, the little girl blacked out and was taken to the emergency room. Treatment failed to revive her, and she slipped into a coma. Weeks later she began a slow recovery, but doctors discovered she had suffered irreversible brain damage and would have to remain in a state institution for the rest of her life. The parents were found guilty of abuse. You are the jury in the case. What punishment do you recommend?

Story 4: A Homicide by Automobile

In the Midwest, a drunk driver's truck hit a busload of elementary school children on their way home from school. The bus overturned in the accident, and five children were killed. Many others were seriously injured—some were paralyzed for life.

The drunk driver was found guilty of manslaughter. You are the jury in the case. What punishment do you recommend?

JUSTICE AND MERCY

Instructions
* Prosecution—List in the "Justice" column as many arguments as you can think of for why the crime deserves the death penalty.
* Defense—List in the "Mercy" column as many arguments as you can think of for why the crime does *not* deserve the death penalty.
* Jury—As you hear the arguments on both sides, write down the arguments that make sense to you in the appropriate columns ("Justice," for the prosecution's arguments; "Mercy," for the defense's arguments).

Justice	**Mercy**
1.	1.
2.	2.
3.	3.
4.	4.
5.	5.
6.	6.
7.	7.
8.	8.
9.	9.
10.	10.

Session 5

Public schools tend to teach evolution as fact, not theory. This is unfortunate not only for Christians, but for anyone seeking scientific truth. That the world evolved is not a provable fact. Proposing it as such violates the basic scientific method. Scientific facts are based on experimental research conducted in controlled conditions producing verifiable evidence that can be reproduced by others using the same controlled conditions. The origin of the world cannot be reproduced in a laboratory.

While true science and Scripture don't disagree, theories like evolution produce some conclusions that contradict biblical truth. How can your young people properly evaluate evolution in the light of the Bible?

How Can Creation Be Right When Practically Everyone Believes in Evolution?

Specific Aims

• To help young people understand that knowing *how* God created us is not nearly as important as knowing *that* He created us; and to affirm that nothing has ever been discovered in science that disproves the biblical account of Creation.

Scriptural Support

• Genesis 1
• Psalm 8

Special Preparation

• Bibles
• Copies of Student Sheet 5-A ("The Foundations of Creation")
• Copies of Student Sheet 5-B ("Here I Stand")
• Pencils
• Chalkboard and chalk or newsprint and marker
• Modeling clay
• Name tags filled in as described in Step 1

1 CREATION PAIRS

Give each group member a name tag with the name of something created on one of the days of Creation. Distribute the name tags so that the six days of creation are equally distributed.

Write one of the following on each name tag to represent each day:

Day 1—Heavens; Earth; Light; Darkness
Day 2—Waters; Sky
Day 3—Dry ground; Seas; Plants; Trees
Day 4—Sun; Moon
Day 5—Land creatures; Sea creatures
Day 6—Male; Female

Ask group members to read Genesis 1 and find one other person with a name tag of something created on the same day as what's written on their name tag.

When everyone has found a partner, give the pairs a lump of clay and instruct them to create a sculpture of something that God created. Encourage the pairs to be creative in their sculptures. After a few minutes, have each pair share its masterpiece with the rest of the group.

2 THE FOUNDATIONS OF CREATION

Distribute a copy of Student Sheet 5-A ("The Foundations of Creation") and a pencil to each pair.

Say something like: **Of course there are many important events and concepts in Genesis 1—after all, it's talking about the beginning of *everything*. But I want you to do something that's going to require a bit of thinking. With your partner, I want you to look through Genesis 1 and decide on what you think are the three most important concepts in the chapter.**

This is strictly your opinion. I'm not asking you to guess what concepts Bible scholars feel are most important; I'm asking you what seems most important to you. When you've decided, write the three concepts and the verses where you found them on your sheet.

Give the pairs several minutes to work. When everyone is finished, have each pair share its three essential concepts. List the ideas on the board as they are presented. If an idea or verse is repeated, put a check mark by the concept already on the list.

When you've done this, focus on the following three concepts:

1. God created (verse 1).
2. God created man—male and female—in His own image (verse 27).
3. Everything that God had created was very good (verse 31).

Say something like: **Obviously, every verse of Genesis 1 is important. This is one of the most important chapters in all the Bible. But let's examine these three specific concepts more closely.**

The fact that God created from nothingness is critically important. Nothing existed before Him. He Himself was not created. He exists infinitely—beyond beginnings and endings. Everything was created by Him. Everything owes its existence to Him.

Secondly, God created human beings after His image. We are the only products of creation that can claim this privilege. This makes us the crown of creation. Read aloud Psalm 8.

Then say something like: **Finally, when God finished creating He saw that His creation was complete, perfect, and good. His perfect design was given to everything in creation.**

Explain to your group members that the purpose of this exercise was to focus their attention on the importance of Genesis 1. Having done that, you can now begin to address the issue of creation vs. evolution.

3 THE HOWS OF CREATION

Ask: **How did God form the earth out of nothingness?**

How did God create living creatures?

How did God form the sun and the moon?

How did God shape male and female from the dust of the earth?

How can the author of Genesis call the first three days of creation, "days," when the sun and moon didn't exist until the fourth day?

After each question, allow time for several group members to offer their opinions.

Then point out that the Scripture doesn't address *how* God created (in modern scientific language) beyond stating boldly that He spoke creation into being.

Ask: **Do you find it hard to believe the account of creation because Scripture doesn't offer specific information about exactly how God did it? Why or why not?**

Do you think more people would believe in creation if the Bible were more detailed about what happened? Why or why not?

Allow time for several group members to respond to these questions.

Then ask: **Why do you suppose the Bible isn't more detailed about creation?** If no one mentions it, point out that the Bible is not a science book; it is a means God uses to communicate His truths to us.

4 PERSONAL BELIEFS

Ask: **What evidence do you know of that supports creation or casts doubts on evolution?**

Use the following to supplement group members' responses:

• **The intricate design and detail of the universe seem to suggest an intelligent Creator.**

• If organisms evolved from simpler ones as evolutionists suggest, there should exist in the fossil record evidence of the various stages of evolution. Instead, there are gaps, or "missing links" in the fossil record that seem to deny the evolution theory.

• One of the basic laws of science is that nature moves from orderliness to chaos; evolution, however, is based on the assumption that nature moves from chaos to orderliness.

Why is it important that we believe the Genesis 1 account of creation? If no one mentions it, point out that, if the Bible is wrong in one area, it could also be wrong in other areas. If God didn't really create the universe as the Bible says, maybe Christ didn't really rise from the dead as the Bible says. To doubt one area of the Bible raises doubts about the entire thing.

Distribute copies of Student Sheet 5-B ("Here I Stand"). Represented on the sheet are a few of the theories Christians hold to concerning the origin of the universe. Instruct group members to read through the sheet and choose the theory that most closely resembles what they believe.

When everyone is finished, ask volunteers to share their responses. Allow time for discussion and debate after each volunteer shares.

Then affirm that it's possible to have different interpretations of Genesis 1— as long as we don't deny the fact that God created everything. The most important thing is not *how* God created, but rather *that* He created.

Have group members form a circle for closing prayer. Ask each person to pray aloud the completion to this phrase: "Father, I'm thankful that you created _____ because . . ."

THE FOUNDATIONS OF CREATION

Read Genesis 1. Then decide which concepts are the most important concerning creation. Write down the three most important concepts in your own words and list the verse in which you found each idea.

CONCEPT 1: _____

_____

Verse: _____

CONCEPT 2: _____

_____

Verse: _____

CONCEPT 3: _____

_____

Verse: _____

Here I Stand

One of the most significant conflicts between biblical creation and evolution is the definition of a "day" and the duration of time needed for creation. What do you believe about creation? Circle the statement that best describes your position.

1. Creation happened in six 24-hour days.

2. God created everything, but over a long period of time. The word "day" in Genesis 1 does not necessarily mean a period of 24 hours. (Second Peter 3:8 says that a day is like 1,000 years to the Lord.)

3. God started the process of creation. Then He allowed life to evolve from the simplest to the most complex organisms.

4. Write your own position if these three don't describe what you believe.

_____

_____

_____

The Bible declares that the love of money is the root of all evil. *Campus Life* magazine reports that 25% of teenagers in the U.S. spend more than $30 of their own money each week. Ninety-three percent of teenage girls say that their favorite pastime is shopping. And 63% of teenagers say that their favorite place to hang out is the mall.

As high school seniors look ahead to a career, they say the most important aspects of a "good job" are "a chance to earn good money" and "the opportunity for advancement and promotion." Materialism dramatically influences teenagers today.

But is the desire to be rich and have a lot of material possessions in direct conflict with being a good Christian?

HOW RICH CAN YOU BE AND STILL BE A GOOD CHRISTIAN?

Specific Aims

• To help group members recognize that all money is a gift from God; to help them understand the principle of giving back to God a portion of what He has given to us; and to help them brainstorm specific ways they can honor God with their money.

Scriptural Support

• Genesis 28:20-22
• Proverbs 10:22; 11:24, 28; 22:1, 4
• Malachi 3:10
• Luke 6:38; 18:18-30
• II Corinthians 9:6-11

Special Preparation

• Bibles
• Copies of Student Sheet 6-A ("Does What You Own, Own You?")
• Copies of Student Sheet 6-B ("Wealth and the Bible")
• Pencils
• Chalkboard and chalk or newsprint and marker
• Paper
• Envelopes

1 HOW RICH ARE WE?

As your group members arrive, distribute copies of Student Sheet 6-A ("Does What You Own, Own You?"). Each person should follow the interview instructions on the sheet. Emphasize to your group members that their goal is to interview as many people as possible. After several minutes, discuss the activity, using the following questions and information.

Do you think young people in our society are too wealthy and spoiled? Why or why not? Encourage group members to compare their lives with what they know of the lives of young people in Third World countries, for example.

If you had to live without three things on the list, what would they be? Go down the list and have group members vote on which three things they would give up. Tally the votes and list the top three vote getters on the board.

What three things on the list would be hardest for you to live without? Go through the list again and have group members vote on the three things that would be hardest for them to live without. Again list the top three vote getters on the board. Then discuss why group members feel these items are so important.

Then say something like: **There was a man in the Bible who also found it difficult to live without some possessions. Let's take a look at his story.** Have everyone read silently the story of the rich ruler in Luke 18:18-30.

When everyone is finished, ask: **Why couldn't the rich ruler part with his wealth?** (Perhaps because it was the most important thing in his life, his "security blanket.")

If Christ asked you to do what He asked the rich ruler to do, would you? Why or why not? Encourage group members to consider carefully what Christ asked before they respond. Would they be willing to give up *everything,* if He asked them to?

Do you think it would be any easier for you than it would have been for the rich ruler? Why or why not? Encourage several group members to respond honestly to these questions.

2 WHERE DOES OUR WEALTH GO?

Label the four corners of the room according to the multiple choice answers to the following questions. Then instruct the group members to go to the corner of the room that corresponds to their answers to the questions. If the group members determine that none of the choices correspond to their answers, instruct them to go to the middle of the room.

#1—On the average, how much of your own money do you spend each week on things just for you?
  a. $5
  b. $10
  c. $20
  d. More than $30

#2—On the average, which items do you spend the most money on each month?

    a. Personal grooming

    b. Clothes

    c. Entertainment and food

    d. Gasoline and car expenses

#3—If you were given $500 right now, what would you do with most of it?

    a. Put it into savings.

    b. Buy clothes.

    c. Buy or do something fun.

    d. Buy gifts for people or give the money to charities.

After group members go to their respective corners for each question, ask volunteers to discuss their responses. How do they feel about the fact that they spend so much on themselves? Why do they spend most of their money on entertainment and food (or something else)? How could they spend $500 on clothes?

Be careful not to make group members defensive in responding to the questions. You're not necessarily judging their spending habits; you're trying to understand those habits.

Ask: **Where should God fit into how we spend our money?** Allow several group members to respond. Then point out that everything we have comes from God. We have a responsibility to return at least a portion back to Him.

3 WEALTH AND THE BIBLE

Before the session, cut apart copies of Student Sheet 6-B ("Wealth and the Bible"). Keep the "Beginnings" cards together and the "Endings" cards together, but make sure the cards within each category are well-shuffled.

Instruct group members to form teams of four. Distribute a set of "Beginnings" cards and a set of "Endings" cards to each team. Give the teams five minutes to match each "beginning" of a Bible verse with its appropriate "ending." However, the teams may not use Bibles to match the cards.

Give the teams a few minutes to check their answers in the Bible and correct any verses that they have wrong. Then briefly discuss each verse, and the principles it presents regarding a Christian's relationship to money. Use the following information to supplement your discussion of the verses.

Luke 6:38—The degree to which you show kindness to others—whether through financial means or in some other manner—is the degree to which you will receive kindness. This is an example of the "What you sow is what you will reap" principle.

Genesis 28: 20-22—Many people believe that this passage (and others like it) sets the example for tithing—giving at least 10% of what we earn back to God for use in His work.

Proverbs 10:22—Wealth is solely a gift from God, and not the result of human deeds. When God's wealth is used God's way, there is no problem with having money.

Proverbs 11:28—If our faith is in our financial well-being instead of in God, we will fall.

Proverbs 11:24—Generosity is the key to blessing and prosperity. The more we give, the more we receive in return. Those who are selfish with their money will "come to poverty."

Proverbs 22:1—Reputation and integrity are much more valuable than riches.

Proverbs 22:4—Humility and fear of the Lord can only be achieved through a personal relationship with Him. That personal relationship will bring us the wealth and honor we need.

Malachi 3:10—The Lord invites His people to test the fact that He will provide them with blessings beyond their imaginations if they follow His principles for handling money.

II Corinthians 9:7—Giving to the Lord should not be done because a person feels he or she *has* to give; it should be done cheerfully, with a desire to honor God with the money He has provided.

Instruct each team to share together completions to the following sentences. Make sure everyone on each team completes each sentence. The sentences are as follows:

One problem with being rich and being a Christian would be . . .

One blessing from being rich and a Christian would be . . .

One way I can use my money for God is . . .

After the teams have had several minutes to share, ask volunteers from each team to share their responses with the rest of the group.

4 RIGHTEOUS AND WICKED USES OF MONEY

Draw two columns on the board. Label one column, "Righteous Person" and the other column, "Wicked Person."

Say something like: **Let's imagine that a righteous person and a wicked person both win the Million Dollar Sweepstakes. In your teams, come up with several ways you believe a wicked person would use the money.** Give the teams a few minutes to do this. Then ask the teams to share what they came up with as you write responses on the board under the "Wicked Person" column.

Then say: **Now list some of the uses a righteous person will find for the million dollars.** Give the teams a few minutes to work. Then list the teams' responses on the board under the "Righteous Person" column as group members call them out.

Discuss why the teams suggested what they did for each column. Why do they think a wicked person would spend money that way? How is the righteous person's use of money different from the wicked person's?

Read aloud II Corinthians 9:6-11. Say something like: **Paul says here that God meets our needs and blesses us so that we may give to meet the needs of others. Think about that. Are you able to give generously and cheerfully to others?**

Suppose God blessed you with a million dollars. Would you be more or less generous with it than with the money you have now?

How would you use a million dollars for the Lord?

Encourage several group members to respond honestly to these questions.

Then say something like: **Let's point out on the righteous person's list all the ways we listed which will bless others.** Go over the list in light of II Corinthians 9:6-11.

Distribute paper, envelopes, and pencils. Ask group members to write down one way they will use their money for the Lord in the coming weeks. Then have group members sign their papers, seal them in the envelopes, and write their addresses on the front of the envelopes. Collect the envelopes and tell group members that you will mail the papers to them in two weeks as reminders of their commitments.

Close the session in prayer, asking God to help your group members as they attempt to honor Him with their money.

Does What You Own, Own You?

Interview as many people in the group as you can. Find out how many of your fellow group members own the following items. As you interview, place a check mark beside each item that is owned by the person you're interviewing. Try to interview everyone in the group, if possible.

POSSESSION	*HOW MANY GROUP MEMBERS OWN IT?*

Bike

Portable stereo/
cassette player

Watch

Home stereo system

A collection of records,
tapes, or CD's

Television

Telephone

Camera

Typewriter

Computer or computer
game system

Car or motorcycle

Over $100 worth of
rings/jewelry

Sporting equipment
worth over $100

Hobby equipment
(baseball cards, stamps,
dolls, collectibles) worth
over $100

Wealth and the Bible

Beginnings	Endings
"Give, and it will be given to you. . . .	. . . For with the measure you use, it will be measured to you" (Luke 6:38).
"Then Jacob made a vow, saying, 'If God will be with me and will watch over me . . .	. . . all that you give me I will give You a tenth" (Genesis 28:20-22).
"The blessing of the Lord brings wealth . . .	. . . and He adds no trouble to it" (Proverbs 10:22).
"Whoever trusts in his riches will fall . . .	. . . but the righteous will thrive like a green leaf" (Proverbs 11:28).
"One man gives freely, yet gains even more . . .	. . . another withholds unduly, but comes to poverty" (Proverbs 11:24).
"A good name . . .	. . . is better than silver or gold" (Proverbs 22:1).
"Humility and the fear of the Lord . . .	. . . bring wealth and honor and life" (Proverbs 22:4).
"'Bring the whole tithe into the storehouse, that there may be food in my house. . . .	. . . Test me in this,' says the Lord Almighty, 'and see if I will not throw open the floodgates of heaven and pour out so much blessing that you will not have room enough for it'"(Malachi 3:10).
"Each man should give what he has decided in his heart to give . . .	. . . not reluctantly or under compulsion, for God loves a cheerful giver" (II Corinthians 9:7).

Sixty-five percent of teenagers have part-time jobs. Many of these jobs are in the fast food or retailing industries. They often require working weekend hours, including Sundays, that full-time employees want off.

Having to work on Sundays is a real issue for many teenagers. If they're not required to work Sunday mornings, they may have to work Sunday afternoons or evenings, causing them to miss youth group activities or evening worship services.

Should a Christian work at all on Sundays? And if a Christian *has* to work on Sundays, should he or she try to arrange a schedule that allows attending morning or evening worship services? And beyond that, does God require a day of rest for us each week?

IS IT WRONG FOR A CHRISTIAN TO WORK ON SUNDAY?

Specific Aims
• To help group members understand why, in Christian tradition, Sunday is set aside as a day to honor God; and to help kids determine whether they can honor God and still work on Sunday.

Scriptural Support
• Exodus 20:8-11
• Deuteronomy 5:12-15
• Nehemiah 13:15-22
• Psalm 46:10; 136
• Ezekiel 20:12-16
• Matthew 12:1-8
• Mark 2:27
• Luke 13:10-17; 14:1-6
• John 5:5-15

Special Preparation
• Bibles
• Copies of Student Sheet 7-A ("What Would I Do?")
• Copies of Student Sheet 7-B ("Honoring God")
• Pencils
• Chalkboard and chalk or newsprint and marker
• Paper
• Index cards with Scripture references written on them, as described in the "Remember the Sabbath" section
• Panel guests

1 How Do You Spend Your Sundays?

Before the session, ask several people from your church to act as a "guest panel." If possible, try to include a wide range of ages among the people on your panel—college students, parents of high schoolers, senior citizens, etc.

Open the session by saying something like: **Today we're going to be talking about how to spend our Sundays. And we're fortunate enough to have some guests with us to help us examine the issue.**

Introduce your guests and ask them to share briefly about how they spend their Sundays. After each guest has had a chance to share, open the floor for questions from your group members. Use the following as needed to supplement your group members' questions.

Do you try to make Sunday a day of relaxation? If so, what kinds of things can interrupt your relaxation? How do you deal with those interruptions? Do you ever have to rearrange your schedule during the week to insure that Sunday is a day of relaxation?

Are there things you won't do on Sundays that you'll do on other days of the week?

Do you think businesses should be open on Sundays?

Do you ever have to work on Sundays? If so, how do you feel about it?

You may want to provide for your guests a copy of some of the questions you'll be asking them, so they'll come to the meeting prepared to answer.

After the interviews, thank your guests for coming, give them a round of applause, and dismiss them.

Afterward, ask several group members to tell about how they usually spend Sundays and why.

Then ask: **How many of you have jobs that require you to work on Sundays** *occasionally*? **How do you feel about that? Does it bother you?**

How many of you have jobs that require you to work *every* **Sunday? How do you feel about that? Does it bother you?**

If a person has a choice, should he or she always choose not to work on Sunday?

Encourage several group members to respond to these questions. Create an open atmosphere for your group members so they'll feel free to share without worrying about your response.

2 What Would I Do?

Distribute copies of Student Sheet 7-A ("What Would I Do?") and pencils. Have group members form pairs and share with their partners what they would do in each situation.

Give the pairs a few minutes to work. Then discuss the situations as a group, using the following questions.

Which situation was hardest for you to decide on? What was hard about it?

What would be a good solution to each situation? Ask several volunteers to share their solutions to each situation.

If you decided to work on a Sunday, how would you make time to worship the Lord?

If you worked on Sunday, what explanations would you give your parents, your youth minister or sponsor, your choir director, etc.? What explanation would you give in prayer to God?

3 REMEMBER THE SABBATH

Read aloud Exodus 20:8-11. Explain that the sabbath, in Jewish tradition, is actually Saturday.

Ask: **Why do so many Christians today honor Sunday as the Lord's Day, instead of Saturday?** (Early Christians worshiped on Sunday because Sunday was the day of Jesus' resurrection. The tradition has continued since then.)

Does the commandment to honor the sabbath apply to Sunday for Christians? Explain that many Christians disagree as to whether the sabbath applies to Sunday or not.

Then say: **Let's look at what the Bible has to say about worship and the Lord's Day.**

Distribute copies of Student Sheet 7-B ("Honoring God"). Have group members form teams of four. Instruct the teams to work together in deciding what honors the Lord on Sunday and what does not.

Give the teams several minutes to work; then have them report their conclusions to the rest of the group. Keep track on the board of which items are circled most often and which are crossed through most often.

Then discuss as a group the activities that people were unsure of.

For the next exercise, you'll need four index cards with the following references written on them:

Card #1—Mark 2:27; Luke 13:10-17; Luke 14:1-6
Card #2—John 5:5-15; Matthew 12:1-8
Card #3—Nehemiah 13:15-22; Ezekiel 20:12-16
Card #4—Exodus 20:8-11; Deuteronomy 5:12-15

Distribute one of the cards to each team. (If your group is small, you may need to give some teams more than one card.) Instruct each team to read the Scripture passages on its card and make a list on the back of Student Sheet 7-B of what the passages say about the sabbath.

Allow several minutes for the teams to work. When everyone is finished, have each team share its findings.

Use the following information to supplement your discussion of the passages.

Team #1—Jesus was pointing out to the Pharisees the hypocrisy of legalistic interpretations of the sabbath laws. Everyone does *some* kind of work every day. Jesus compared rescuing a son or an ox that had fallen into a well—"emergency work"—with the healing He performed on the sabbath.

Team #2—Jesus was pointing out that the sabbath did not take precedence over the necessities of life. The disciples were hungry, so they picked the grain to eat. Their "work" did not violate the sabbath laws. Neither did the man who picked up His mat and walked as Jesus had commanded him. Since Jesus is Lord of the sabbath, His commands take precedence over the sabbath laws.

Team #3—Nehemiah, acting in accordance with the sabbath laws, prevented outside merchants from coming into Jerusalem and selling their wares on the sabbath. And, as punishment for openly defying the sabbath laws, the Israelites were not permitted to enter the promised land. In fact, the entire nation was almost destroyed because of their treatment of the sabbath. Both of these accounts emphasize the importance of the sabbath laws to the Jews.

Team #4—The Israelites were not to do any kind of physical labor on the sabbath. They were to treat it as a day of rest in remembrance of God's work during Creation and His work in rescuing them from Egypt.

Instruct group members to look back at Student Sheet 7-B. Ask: **In light of the passages we just looked at, would you change your mind about whether some of these activities are OK to do on Sundays?** Encourage group members to rethink their answers carefully. Ask for volunteers to respond.

Then ask: **What would you say is the most important principle the Bible teaches about remembering the Lord's Day?** Allow plenty of time for group members to respond.

Then say something like: **The sabbath seems to have been created for two important reasons: worshiping God and resting people. Each week, whenever we fail to do both of these things, we violate the will of God. The sabbath is more than just a day—it's a time set aside for God. As Psalm 46:10 says, "Be still, and know that I am God." Whenever our lives become too busy for stillness, rest, and worship, we have the wrong priorities for our time.**

In closing, read Psalm 136 responsively—you read each verse and have your group members read the response, "His love endures forever."

Close the session in prayer.

What Would I Do?

Situation #1

You work for a fast food restaurant. When you were hired, the supervisor promised you at least every other Sunday off. Since then, some people at the restaurant have quit. To take up the slack, you're now being scheduled to work every Sunday, and you're not able to go to worship services or youth group activities. What do you do?

Situation #2

You've just bought a car. Now, in addition to your payments, you need money for gas and insurance. Your old job never required you to work on Sundays. But, with your need for extra income, the only time you can work more is Sundays. You hear that a store at the mall is hiring teenagers to work Sunday-only shifts. What do you do?

Situation #3

You are president of your youth group, and you also help usher during worship services on Sunday mornings. You've just gotten a new job that requires you to work some Sundays. As a result, you'll be missing a lot of youth meetings and worship services. You were just asked to help teach the third grade Sunday school class. You plan to go into church work in the future and would love this opportunity to teach. What do you do?

Honoring God

Circle the activities that you believe could honor God on Sundays.

Draw a line through the activities that you feel would not honor God on Sundays.

Put a question mark beside the activities that you are unsure about.

1. Selling alcohol on Sunday.

2. Opening any store on Sunday.

3. Opening only food stores and gasoline stations on Sunday.

4. Working on Sunday to earn extra money for luxuries.

5. Working on Sunday at essential jobs like community services, hospitals, etc.

6. Going to football games on Sunday.

7. Worshiping in church on Sunday.

8. Going on family outings on Sunday.

9. Going to the mall on Sunday.

10. Eating out at a restaurant on Sunday.

11. Staying at home and doing nothing on Sunday.

Session 8

When President Bush called for military action in the Persian Gulf, a generation of Christian young people was suddenly faced with a dilemma that had been absent from the U.S. since the last days of Viet Nam. *What is my responsibility to the defense of my country—and how does that conflict with my responsibility to God?*

Most people who join the military are taught that, in fulfilling their duties, they may be required to kill or die for their country. Does that mindset fit into the Christian belief system?

Of course God commands us not to murder; but the Old Testament records several instances in which God commanded His chosen people, Israel, to go to war and kill entire populations. Was that part of the Old Testament system that was abolished when Christ came? Or is war still a justifiable cause for killing?

SHOULD A CHRISTIAN SERVE IN THE MILITARY?

Specific Aim

• To help group members recognize that they have a responsibility to both God and country, but, in areas of conflict, God always takes precedence; and to help them understand both sides of the pacifism issue.

Scriptural Support

• Genesis 12:2, 3
• Exodus 14:13, 14
• I Samuel 15:1-3
• Isaiah 2:4
• Matthew 5:43-48
• Luke 12:4, 5
• Romans 13:1-7

Special Preparation

• Bibles
• Copies of Student Sheet 8-A ("Hawks and Doves")
• Copies of Student Sheet 8-B ("Dear Diary")
• Pencils
• Chalkboard and chalk or newsprint and marker
• Paper
• List of veterans and those in military service from your church

1 WOULD YOU GO TO WAR?

Before the session, cut up several copies of Student Sheet 8-A ("Hawks and Doves") into four cards. As group members arrive, hand each of them a card. Make sure that the four different categories of cards are more or less equally distributed. Instruct group members to form four groups, according to the categories on their cards.

Say something like: **The world is on the brink of war. A Middle East country has just invaded Taman and taken control of all of Taman's oil fields. Since most of the oil imported to the United States comes from Taman, the U.S., as well as most of the free world, is threatened.**

The hostile country is threatening to cut off all oil to the West if western nations do not meet certain demands. The demands include outrageously high prices for oil.

American military forces are on full alert. The United States has only 24 hours to agree to the demands before the invaders start killing Americans trapped in Taman. Based on the beliefs written on your cards, what do you think should be done?

Instruct the four groups to discuss the crisis among themselves and determine what they think should be done. Emphasize that each group's opinion should be based solely on the information on its cards, and should not reflect the personal opinions of the group members.

When all four groups have reached a conclusion, combine the two "Hawks" groups to form one team; and combine the two "Doves" groups to form another team. Instruct both teams to combine the resources, information, and reasoning of its various groups to generate material for a debate between the Hawks and the Doves. The Hawks will argue for war; the Doves will argue for pacifism.

Allow several minutes for the two teams to prepare their debate arguments and defense. As one team presents its arguments, the other team should write down questions to attack that position.

After the initial presentations, give the teams an opportunity to question one another, as well as the opportunity to respond to questions.

After the debate, discuss these questions:

How did you feel about the role position you were given? Did that position coincide with your personal beliefs? If so, how did it coincide? If not, how did it differ?

When your side was being challenged and questioned, what were you thinking and feeling?

Allow time for several group members to respond to these questions.

2 HERE I STAND

Say something like: **Over the centuries, well-meaning Christians have been on both sides of the war and peace issue. The Amish and Quakers, among oth-**

ers, refuse to serve in the military because of their Christian beliefs. Other Christians insist that just wars should be waged against forces of evil such as the armies of Hitler and Saddam Hussein.

Let's look more closely at what Scripture says about the pacifism/war issue. Have a volunteer from each of the four groups in the previous exercise read aloud the Bible passages listed on his or her group's card.

After each volunteer finishes, discuss the passage(s). Use the following information to supplement your discussion.

Hawk #1

Genesis 12:2, 3; I Samuel 15:1-3—When God made the covenant with Abram that established the nation of Israel, He promised to bless those who bless Israel and curse those who curse Israel. Some would say that America, in aligning itself with Israel during a time of war, sets itself up to receive God's blessing. Others would say that this blessing may not apply to the modern, secular state of Israel.

It would appear that God's commandment, "You shall not kill," was not to be applied during wars in the Old Testament. The Old Testament records many instances of God commanding the Israelites to invade a territory and kill inhabitants. Christians disagree today whether the commandment applies in war today.

Hawk #2

Romans 13:1-7—Many Christians feel our responsibility to submit to government authority includes a responsibility to fulfill military duty when called upon to do so. If our government determines that a war is necessary and institutes a draft, these Christians would say, our responsibility would be to comply. For some people, this sense of responsibility to government may involve enlisting in the military, even during a time of peace.

Still other Christians believe that military service is not for believers, citing the instruction to "obey God rather than men" (Acts 5:29). If drafted, some of these believers might serve in non-combat roles (such as medics) or might declare "conscientious objector" status. Some, if not allowed these alternatives, have been willing to go to jail for their beliefs.

Dove #1

Matthew 5:43-48; Luke 12:4, 5—Jesus' command to love our enemies and pray for those who persecute us seems to contradict the idea of war. Some Christians, therefore, refuse to fight. Others say that loving our enemies, at some point, may involve preventing them from harming us and others. God may answer our prayers, these Christians say, by using us as instruments to prevent the spread of evil.

Dove #2

Exodus 14:13, 14; Isaiah 2:4—Of course the Lord can take care of any battle; He doesn't *need* our help. He will judge as He sees fit. But some Christians say we still must make ourselves available, in case He desires to use us in fighting a just war.

Sum up the discussion with the following:

Some Christians say that our ultimate goal is the day when no more war is necessary, when Christ's judgments will settle disputes among nations. But until that time, just war will remain the final option for halting the spread of evil in the world.

Other Christians say that following Christ's commands and example require us to reject war. The consequences may be fatal (as other kinds of obedience can be), but these believers would say that nonviolence is the best option because they believe it is the biblical one.

Ask: **Based on what we've talked about, where do you stand on the issue of Christians serving in the military and fighting in a war?**

Would you enlist in the military during a non-war time?

Encourage several volunteers to respond to these questions.

Then ask: **If you were drafted to fight in a war, would you go? Why or why not?**

Would you declare yourself a conscientious objector—someone who refuses to fight in a war because of religious beliefs?

Would you volunteer to serve in the military in a non-combat position?

Distribute copies of Student Sheet 8-B ("Dear Diary") and pencils. Say something like: **Imagine that this is a page from your diary. You've just received notice that you've been drafted into the military to serve and possibly fight for your country. Write in your diary what you will do and why.**

When everyone is finished, ask volunteers to share what they wrote. Briefly discuss their decisions and reasoning. Don't force anyone to share here; after all, these are "diary entries."

3 PRAYER FOR THE TROOPS

Say something like: **Jesus tells us that there will always be wars and rumors of wars. There is a possibility that some people in this room will fight, and even die, in a war.**

Do any of you know of someone who is currently serving in the military, someone who is a veteran of a war, or someone who died in a war? As group members offer names, write the names on the board.

Before the session, you'll need to compile your own list of people in the church who are currently serving in the military, who are veterans of war, or who died in a war. Use your list to supplement your group members' list.

Then say: **Let's take a moment and pray for these people and their families.**

Pause for a few minutes of silent prayer. Then close the session by praying for peace in the world.

Hawks and Doves

Hawk #1

You believe that any enemy of the United States and Israel is an enemy of God. Just as God used Israel, His chosen people, to destroy its enemies in the Old Testament, so today God requires that we go to war and destroy our enemies.

See Genesis 12:2, 3 and I Samuel 15:1-3.

Hawk #2

You believe that governments and armies were instituted by God to protect us. As such, the armies of the world need to defeat this lawless dictator and establish peace, justice, and order again. A just war is necessary to defeat this evil leader in the same way Hitler was defeated in World War II.

See Romans 13:1-7.

Dove #1

You believe that we should forgive our enemies and do good to those who attack us. We must turn the other cheek to this dictator, even if it means that his armies physically destroy us. We have no need to fear people who can only destroy us physically.

See Matthew 5:43-48 and Luke 12:4, 5.

Dove #2

You believe that all war is wrong. We should take all of our weapons and destroy them. God will take care of the evildoers if we simply obey Him. He will see that justice is done—if not in this life, certainly in the next.

See Exodus 14:13, 14 and Isaiah 2:4.

DEAR DIARY

Dear Diary,

Today I received a draft notice.

Session 9

Movies and books dealing with demons and the occult are quite popular—especially with teenagers. There has also been a marked increase in interest in the "spiritual" side of the occult—tarot cards, astrology, etc. Teenagers are also on the forefront of this trend.

There is something fascinating about "the dark side." And as Christian teens begin to delve into that dark side, they're going to face things they may not be ready for. A knowledge of the nature and work of demons may go a long way in preventing serious trouble for your group members in the future.

CAN A CHRISTIAN BE DEMON-POSSESSED?

Specific Aims

• To help young people recognize that demons are a real force in the world—and that Christians can be *oppressed* by them, but that if we have the Holy Spirit in our lives, demons cannot *own* us.

Scriptural Support

• Deuteronomy 18:10
• Matthew 10:1; 25:41
• Luke 8:26-33; 11:24-26
• Acts 8:9-25; 19:15
• Romans 8:37-39

• Ephesians 6:10-18
• James 4:7
• I Peter 5:8
• II Peter 2:4
• I John 4:4

Special Preparation

• Bibles
• Copies of Student Sheet 9-A ("Do Demons Exist?")
• Copies of Student Sheet 9-B ("The Uninvited")
• Pencils
• Paper
• Chalkboard and chalk or newsprint and marker
• Couch or six folding chairs
• Newspapers
• Three cups filled with dirt
• Three empty cups
• Broom
• Dustpan
• Two water pitchers—one empty and one filled with water
• Stool or small table
• Name placards with string or yarn tied to them so that they can be hung around the actors' necks

1 DO DEMONS EXIST?

Open the session by asking: **Do you believe in leprechauns?**
Do you believe in Santa Claus?
Do you believe in the Easter Bunny?
Do you believe in aliens from other planets?
Do you believe in demons? Allow time for group members to offer their opinions.

Then ask: **When you think of a demon, what image comes to mind? What does it look like? What does it do?** Again allow time for group members to offer their opinions.

How do the media portray demons and satanic activity? Think of all the movies, books, songs, or rock groups that you're aware of that focus on evil, the satanic, or the demonic.

As group members suggest movies, books, songs, and bands, make a list of their suggestions on the board. Supplement their responses by suggesting movies like *The Exorcist, Hellraiser,* and *Ghostbusters*; most books by Stephen King, including *Christine* and *Children of the Corn*; and songs by groups like AC/DC, Black Sabbath, and Ozzy Osbourne.

After making the list, ask: **Do you think these movie makers, authors, and musicians believe in the devil and demons?**

What is the appeal of movies, songs, and books that focus on satanic or demonic activities?

Do you think Christians should watch these movies, read these books, or listen to this music?

Allow time for several group members to respond to these questions. Encourage discussion and debate. You're not necessarily looking for "right" answers here; you're just looking for group members' opinions.

2 SHEDDING SOME LIGHT ON THE DARK SIDE

Say something like: **The Bible has a lot to say about Satan, demons, witchcraft, and the occult.**

Distribute copies of Student Sheet 9-A ("Do Demons Exist?") and pencils. Give group members several minutes to complete the survey. Then have group members form pairs and compare answers with their partners. After comparing responses, have the pairs change any answers they believe might be wrong.

Write the following Scripture references on the board:
1. II Peter 2:4
2. Luke 8:26-33
3. Luke 8:30
4. Acts 19:15
5. Matthew 10:1

6. Deuteronomy 18:10
7. Acts 8:9-25
8. I Peter 5:8
9. Ephesians 6:10-18
10. James 4:7
11. Matthew 25:41

Instruct each pair to check its answers by looking up the passages on the board. When everyone is finished, go over the correct answers as a group.

The correct answers are as follows—1. True; 2. True; 3. False; 4. True; 5. False (but it has to be done in His name); 6. True; 7. False; 8. True; 9. False; 10. True; 11. True.

When you've finished the quiz, distribute paper and pencils to each pair. Instruct the pairs to come up with revised descriptions of what a demon is like, based on the passages you just looked at. Give the pairs several minutes to work; then have volunteers share their descriptions with the rest of the group.

3 THE UNINVITED

Say something like: **In the Middle Ages, "morality plays" were used to teach the truths of God. Since many people in those days could not read the Bible, morality plays would act out biblical truths so the people could see and learn them. We're going to perform a morality play based on Luke 11:24-26 to answer the question, "Is it possible for a Christian to be demon-possessed?"**

This play requires six people. (You will need to serve as "Narrator.") Distribute a copy of Student Sheet 9-B ("The Uninvited") to each actor. Before the session, make name placards for every character in the play. The placards should be made so that they can be hung around the actors' necks. Explain to your group members that the placards are necessary for character identification since you do not have costumes. Before the session, make sure you have the necessary props for the scenes.

The characters are as follows:
A. Person
Demon #1
Demon #2
Demon #3
Holy Spirit
Armor of God

Designate an area of the room to be the stage by spreading newspaper on the floor. Put in the middle of the stage a couch or several chairs in a row. Explain that the newspaper area represents a person's life.

Assign the roles and distribute the name placards accordingly. Then say something like: **Read each scene through once. Look at your part and then think how you will pantomime the scene.**

Give the actors an opportunity to read through each scene. Then have them present the play. When they are finished, give them a round of applause.

Discuss the play briefly, using the following questions.

Why was it so hard to keep the demons from coming back into the person? (Nothing had replaced the demon in the person's life when the demon left; there was a void waiting to be filled. So nothing stood in the demon's way when it came back.)

Explain that you're not saying all or even many non-Christians are demon-possessed. But those without the Holy Spirit are more vulnerable to attack by the devil.

What does the person need to keep demons from taking possession? (The Holy Spirit and the armor of God.)

Point out that, if we have the Holy Spirit in our lives, demons cannot *own* us. However, Christians must still avoid "letting their guards down."

Read aloud James 4:7.

Say something like: **Even after we have the Holy Spirit in our lives, the devil is still a force to be reckoned with—and a force to be resisted.**

What does it mean to 'resist the devil'? (Responses might include: avoid demonic/satanic music, movies, literature; pray for strength during times of temptation, etc.)

According to James 4:7, what will happen if we resist the devil? (He will flee from us.)

Have group members form a circle for closing prayer. Announce that your closing prayer is taken from I John 4:4—"The One who is in you is greater than the one who is in the world." Have your group members recite the phrase in unison.

Do Demons Exist?

If one of the following statements agrees with the Bible's teachings on Satan, demons, and the occult, circle "T" for true. If the statement does not agree with Scripture, circle "F" for false.

T or F   1. The demons of hell are fallen angels who rebelled against God.

T or F   2. People or animals can be demon-possessed.

T or F   3. An unbeliever can be possessed by only one demon at a time.

T or F   4. Demons recognize who Jesus is.

T or F   5. Only Jesus is able to cast out evil spirits.

T or F   6. The practices of witchcraft and the occult are forbidden by the Bible.

T or F   7. Certain believers in the Bible were owned and controlled by evil spirits.

T or F   8. Satan attacks and seeks to destroy believers.

T or F   9. The Christian can do nothing to resist the attacks of Satan.

T or F   10. Satan fears and is powerless against believers who resist him.

T or F   11. Eternal judgment and fire are reserved for Satan and his demonic angels.

THE UNINVITED

ACT 1

Narrator: **Once there was a person named A. Person.** [A. Person enters and stands next to the couch/row of chairs.] **Sadly, within this well-meaning person dwelled an evil spirit named Demon #1.** [Demon #1 enters and sits in the middle of the stage, acting as if he or she owns the place—being very arrogant and smug. He or she dumps a cup of dirt on the newspaper and starts spreading it around.]

A. Person tried very hard to live a good life. But the demon inside him kept spreading dirt throughout his life. Finally, A. Person decided that enough was enough and swept the demon out of his life. [A. Person takes a broom and begins to sweep up the dirt. Then he throws Demon #1 out.]

ACT 2

[Demon #2 and Demon #3 stand in a corner of the room, opposite the newspaper area. Each demon is holding a cup of dirt and an empty cup. The demons are trying to party, but are very hot and thirsty. They attempt to drink from their cups, but find there is no water. They try to fill their cups from an empty water pitcher, but find there is no water. Demon #1 joins them. At the same time, A. Person is sweeping up the dirt on the newspaper.]

Narrator: **Now that the evil spirit is gone, A. Person cleans up his life. Sweeping out all the dirt, he tries to be really good. He tells himself over and over again that he will "see no evil," "hear no evil," and "do no evil."**

But even though his life has been cleaned up, he is empty inside. Demon #1, meanwhile, went into a dry, arid place, and found nowhere to rest. So he returns to spy on A. Person to see if anything has filled the void in the person's life. [Demon #1 sneaks around, checking out the condition of A. Person.]

ACT 3

A. Person: [Places both hands over his eyes and chants repeatedly] **I see no evil.** [Places both hands over his ears and chants repeatedly] **I hear no evil.** [Folds both arms across his chest and chants repeatedly] **I do no evil.**

Narrator: **A. Person did not fill the void in his life with the Holy Spirit. Demon #1 saw this and invited two other demons to join him for a party inside A. Person's life.**

The demons overwhelmed him. Relaxing inside in his home, they spread their dirt throughout and partied to their hearts' content. [Demons walk onto the newspaper, sit on the couch or chairs, fill their empty cups with water, and spread dirt around on the newspaper. They act as if they are having a great time partying. They also laugh at and make fun of A. Person.]

Act 4

[A. Person stands in the middle of the stage.]

Narrator: **When a person accepts Jesus Christ as Lord and Savior, that person receives the gift of the indwelling of the Holy Spirit.** [The Holy Spirit enters and stands next to A. Person.] **The Holy Spirit then encourages A. Person to be alert, to pray always, and to stand firm.**

Holy Spirit: [to A. Person he whispers repeatedly] **Be alert. Pray always. Stand firm.**

Narrator: **The Holy Spirit also encourages the Christian to put on the whole armor of God.** [Holy Spirit motions for Armor of God. Armor of God enters and stands next to A. Person like a bodyguard.] **The demons again try to take ownership.** [Demons #1-3 enter and try to take over the newspaper area, but Armor of God, the Holy Spirit, and A. Person form such a strong barricade, the demons are unable to get past them.] **If we use the armor of God, there is no way for the demons to take over. While they may harass and attack, they cannot possess the obedient Christian.** [Demons give up and leave.]

Romans 8:37-39 says, "No, in all these things we are more than conquerors through Him who loved us. For I am convinced that neither death nor life, neither angels nor demons, neither the present nor the future, nor any powers, neither height nor depth, nor anything else in all creation, will be able to separate us from the love of God that is in Christ Jesus our Lord."

Session 10

The death of a loved one is a traumatic experience for any young person. But if that loved one was not a Christian, the trauma is multiplied. In such cases, even the most faithful Christians can be moved to question God's plan for salvation and eternal judgment.

If a recent death of a non-Christian has prompted this session, exercise sensitivity as you present the material. You want to give kids the biblical facts concerning our eternal destiny; but you want to avoid compounding the grief of affected group members.

HOW COULD GOD SEND GOOD PEOPLE TO HELL?

Specific Aims

• To help group members understand that, because of our sin, we all deserve to be punished; to help them recognize the mercy God shows us by providing His Son as a means for us to escape hell; and to help them understand that people who choose to live without God in this life are choosing to live apart from Him in the next.

Scriptural Support

• Isaiah 64:6
• Matthew 10:32, 33; 18:10; 25:31-46
• Mark 10:13-15
• Luke 13:24-30; 16:19-31; 18:16, 17
• John 3:16; 14:6
• Acts 14:11-18

• Romans 1:18-32; 3:10, 12, 23; 4:1-8; 5:6-8; 10:9
• I Corinthians 6:9a
• Ephesians 2:1-3, 8-10
• Hebrews 9:27; 11
• James 2:10
• I John 1:9
• Revelation 20:11-15

Special Preparation

• Bibles
• Copies of Student Sheet 10-A ("So Who's Perfect Anyway?")
• Copies of Student Sheet 10-B ("What about . . . ?")
• Pencils
• Newsprint and markers
• Index cards
• Nails
• Trash can
• A wooden cross made from two 2 x 4's; a hammer (optional)

1 SO WHO'S PERFECT ANYWAY?

Before the session, tape two large sheets of newsprint to the wall. At the top of one sheet write, "Goodness." At the top of the other sheet write, "Perfection."

To begin the session, distribute markers to group members and instruct them to write on the sheets as many words or phrases as they can think of that define each term. Then have them write on the sheets the names of people who exemplify goodness and perfection.

Look at the words and phrases the group members have written. Read the names of the people they chose. (Probably the only names your group members suggested for "Perfection" were God, Jesus, and/or the Holy Spirit.) Discuss why they wrote what they did.

Then ask: **What's the difference between goodness and perfection?** Allow time for several group members to respond. If no one mentions it, explain that the difference between goodness and perfection is the standard of comparison. In other words, any of us can achieve "goodness" when we compare ourselves to another person. There's always somebody else whose actions or lifestyle is worse than ours. So, compared to those people, we're "good." But, if we're trying to achieve perfection, the only person to compare ourselves with is Christ. And in that comparison, we will always come up lacking. Any of us can achieve what society considers goodness; none of us can achieve perfection.

Distribute copies of Student Sheet 10-A ("So Who's Perfect Anyway?") and pencils. Give group members a few minutes to fill out the sheets.

Then say something like: **When we're honest with ourselves and with God, we must confess that we can't measure up to His standard of perfection. Jesus says, "Be perfect . . . as your heavenly Father is perfect." That means that the only way to pass the test we've just taken is to mark "Yes" by every question. And that's impossible. It's impossible to keep all the commandments of God throughout every moment of our lives.**

Goodness is measured in human terms when we compare our lives with other human beings. But when we measure ourselves to God's standard of perfection—Jesus Christ—what do we discover? Let's explore what the Bible says about our condition.

2 NO ONE IS RIGHTEOUS?

Put up two new sheets of newsprint. At the top of one of the sheets write, "The Bad News." At the top of the other sheet write, "The Good News."

Assign the following Scripture passages to six volunteers: Isaiah 64:6; Romans 3:23; Romans 3:10; Romans 3:12; James 2:10; Ephesians 2:1-3.

Instruct the volunteers to read their passages and then write on the "Bad News" sheet the answer to this question: **What does God say about our goodness in this passage?** Write the question on the board for emphasis.

When all the volunteers have written their answers on the sheet, discuss their responses briefly, using the following information.

Isaiah 64:6—We are all unclean; and when we try to become "clean" by doing righteous things, it still looks like filthy rags to God. We are swept away by our sins like a shriveled leaf in the wind.

Romans 3:23—All of us have sinned and fallen far short of God's standard.

Romans 3:10—No one is righteous.

Romans 3:12—Everyone has turned away from God; any "good" work that a person without Christ performs is considered worthless by God.

James 2:10—If a person obeys every law of God for his entire life, but then breaks *one* law *one* time, that person is a law-breaker.

Ephesians 2:1-3—We are spiritually (and eternally) dead in our sins.

Read aloud I Corinthians 6:9a. Then say something like: **The Bible makes it very clear—we are all sinners. And as sinners, we cannot inherit the kingdom of God. So we need something or someone beyond ourselves to make us righteous, to make us eligible to inherit the kingdom of God. Let's look at the "Good News."**

Assign the following Scripture passages to six volunteers: John 3:16; John 14:6; Romans 5:6-8; Romans 10:9; Ephesians 2:8-10; I John 1:9.

Instruct the volunteers to read their passages and then write on the "Good News" sheet the answer to this question: **What does God say about our salvation in this passage?** Write the question on the board for emphasis.

When all the volunteers have written their answers on the sheet, discuss their responses briefly, using the following information.

John 3:16—God loves us so much that, even after we rebelled against Him, He gave us a way—through the sacrifice of His Son—to have eternal life with Him.

John 14:6—There is absolutely no way to get to heaven except through Christ.

Romans 5:6-8—We are powerless to do anything on our own to get to heaven, so God sent His Son to save us.

Romans 10:9—All we have to do to be saved is to confess that Jesus is Lord and believe in His resurrection.

Ephesians 2:8-10—We have absolutely nothing to boast about concerning our salvation. The only thing we have to do to receive salvation is accept it as a gift.

I John 1:9—If we confess our sins, God can always be counted on to forgive us, and to restore us to a righteous relationship with Him.

Say something like: **Righteousness is something we can't achieve on our own. The only way we can become righteous—and enter God's requirement of perfection—is to surrender our lives to the righteous One—Jesus Christ, who shed His blood on the cross for us.**

3 WHAT ABOUT . . . ?

Say something like: **Keeping in mind the Scripture passages and principles we've talked about, answer the following question: Does God send people to hell?** Allow time for several responses. If group members have trouble answering the question, read aloud Matthew 10:32, 33. Then point out that our decision to either accept or reject Jesus determines our eternal destination. God's role is to simply carry out the consequences of our decision.

Instruct group members to form groups of four. Distribute copies of Student Sheet 10-B ("What about . . . ?"). Have the groups fill out the sheet together.

Allow several minutes for group members to work. Then ask for several volunteers to share their responses and explain how their groups reached those conclusions.

Use the following information to supplement your discussion.

#1—The passages indicate that ignorance of God's plan of salvation is no excuse for rejecting Him. In some form or another (i.e., nature—rain, crops, food, etc.), everyone is aware of God. The passages also indicate that everyone is aware, in some form or another, of the consequences of their actions.

#2—The passages imply that little children, too young to understand their need for salvation, will be admitted to the kingdom of God.

#3—Under the Old Testament law, sins were "covered over" through such physical acts as sacrificing animals. Before the death and resurrection of Christ, people became righteous by faith in what God revealed.

#4—If a person dies without receiving Christ as Savior, he or she *immediately* faces judgment. There are no "second chances."

4 THE MOST IMPORTANT PRAYER IN THE WORLD

Say something like: *We* **make the decision on whether heaven or hell is our eternal destiny.**

If you were to die right this moment, are you sure that you would be with Jesus forever? Going to church, youth meetings, or Sunday school doesn't make you a Christian. Only trusting Jesus as Lord and Savior does. He died and shed His blood to forgive and save you—no matter what you've done or said in the past.

I hope you won't leave this room without knowing for sure that you have received Christ as your Savior.

Distribute an index card, a pencil, and a nail to each group member. Say: **Take this card and write on it any sin you need forgiveness for from God.** Give group members a few minutes to do this.

Then say: **Now fold the card over once and push the nail through it.** When group members have done this, instruct them to form a circle around either a trash can or a wooden cross. If you use a wooden cross, have each group member nail his or her card to the cross. If you use a trash can, have each group member simply throw away his or her card.

Then say: **I'm going to pray what's known as the "sinner's prayer." If you've never prayed this prayer before, and would like to have the assurance of being saved by Jesus, repeat to yourself what I pray. God knows your heart. If your prayer is sincere, He will give you eternal life with Jesus. That's His promise. You can count on it.**

Pray the following prayer aloud, pausing after each phrase to allow group members to repeat it to themselves.

Jesus, I surrender my life to you. I am a sinner. I trust you as my Lord and Savior. Jesus, I believe you are God's Son, and my salvation and righteousness. I surrender all of me to You right now. In Your name I pray. Amen.

Make yourself available after the session to group members who want to talk to you in more detail about their commitments.

So Who's Perfect Anyway?

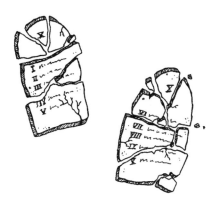

The following questions are based on the Ten Commandments. Read each question and answer it honestly. Your answers will remain private—no one else will see them.

Yes   No   1. Has there ever been a time in your life when you trusted someone or some thing instead of God?

Yes   No   2. Has there ever been a time in your life when you "did your own thing" without asking God first?

Yes   No   3. Have you ever thought or spoken God's name in profanity or cursing?

Yes   No   4. Have you ever treated what the Bible calls the "day of rest" as you would any other day?

Yes   No   5. Has there ever been a time in your life when you dishonored or disobeyed your parents?

Yes   No   6. Jesus says that hating a person is the same as murdering him. Have you ever felt intense dislike or even momentary hate for someone?

Yes   No   7. Have you ever gazed lustfully at someone in person or at someone pictured in a pornographic magazine or in a movie?

Yes   No   8. Have you ever taken something that wasn't yours?

Yes   No   9. Have you ever told a lie or exaggerated a story about someone?

Yes   No   10. Have you ever been envious of something that someone else owned, like a stereo, a car, clothes, etc.?

Total Number of "No's" you circled _____

WHAT ABOUT . . . ?

When people get into a discussion about who's going to heaven or hell, there always seems to be the "What about 'so-and-so'?" questions. Let's see how you would answer these questions. Use the Scripture passages to help you in your decision making.

1. What about people who have never heard the Gospel, like tribe members of some remote village—would they go to hell when they die?
Read Romans 1:18-32; Acts 14:11-18; Revelation 20:11-15; and Matthew 25:31-46.

2. What about babies or children who die before they are old enough to accept Jesus—would they go to hell when they die?
Read Matthew 18:10; Mark 10:13-15; and Luke 18:16, 17.

3. What about the people who lived before Jesus died on the cross—did they go to hell when they died?
Read Hebrews 11 and Romans 4:1-8.

4. What about people who have already died without accepting Christ—will they be given another opportunity?
Read Luke 13:24-30; Luke 16:19-31; and Hebrews 9:27.

Relatively few teenagers would call themselves Satanists. Yet countless junior and senior high students, knowingly or not, are involved in activities that have the evil one as their source.

Deception is a subtle process. Many kids have no idea what's happening to them until it's too late. Case after bizarre case is reported year after year involving young people whose lives are destroyed by occult-related activities. So many cases have turned up in the last several years that police forces across the country have asked experts on the occult for training in dealing with occult-related crimes.

The world of the average teenager today is not the relatively safe place it was when his or her parents were kids. These days, curiosity can be a killer. Helping kids get "clued in" to the danger out there can literally be a matter of life and death.

WHAT'S SO BAD ABOUT PLAYING AROUND WITH THE OCCULT?

Specific Aim
• To warn kids about the powerful pull of the occult; and to help kids recognize that any interest in the occult supplants God in their lives.

Scriptural Support
• Deuteronomy 18:9-14
• II Corinthians 11:14, 15
• Galatians 5:19-24
• Ephesians 6:10-18
• Revelation 20:11–21:8

Special Preparation
• Bibles
• Copies of Student Sheet 11-A ("How Bad is Bad?")
• Copies of Student Sheet 11-B ("The Ouija Board")
• Pencils
• Chalkboard and chalk or newsprint and marker
• Colored pencils or pens
• Paper
• Two hard-boiled eggs and one raw egg (optional)
• A "Mousetrap" game (optional)

1 TRAPS AND TRICKERY

Choose one of the following openers. Your choice probably will depend on whether you can risk pelting one of your kids and your meeting place with a raw egg.

Messy Option

Ask for three volunteers. They should be kids who are wearing casual clothes and are good sports, since they may get a little egg on them (but don't tell them that).

Tell the volunteers and the group: **The object of this game is to see how many hard-boiled eggs these three can keep in the air amongst themselves at the same time. We'll give them one hard-boiled egg to toss around as quickly as possible. Then once each person has touched the egg at least once, we will add another egg. We will keep adding eggs as long as they can keep them all going.**

Put the volunteers in the center of the rest of the group in a triangle, with about six feet between tossers. Give tossers a minute to strategize—figuring out which direction they'll throw the eggs (clockwise or counterclockwise), whether they should all throw after the count of "1, 2, 3," etc.

Once they're ready, hand the first hard-boiled egg to the tosser nearest you and have him or her start the game. As soon as the egg gets all the way around, and the person nearest you tosses it the second time, hand him or her the second hard-boiled egg.

Once the tosser nearest you catches and tosses both the first and second eggs, hand him or her the third egg. But this egg will *not* be hard-boiled—it will be fresh, raw, and fragile. Chances are good that this egg will live a short life, especially if there are three eggs in the air. If the egg survives a couple of times around, dare the tossers to see how fast they can get the eggs going without dropping them.

If and when the egg breaks, act surprised and ask: **What happened?**

If the egg makes it around the triangle several times without breaking, congratulate the tossers and let them and the larger group in on your secret. Say: **There was an imposter among the eggs. One of the eggs was raw, not hard-boiled!** Give the tossers a moment to regain composure or gloat over their confirmed suspicion (they were probably skeptical from the start).

Then ask the tossers: **What would you have done differently if you had known you were tossing a raw egg rather than a hard-boiled one?** ("I wouldn't have volunteered"; "I would have been more careful"; "I would have made sure it broke against one of the other tossers," etc.) If these responses are not offered, suggest them as possibilities before moving on.

Once the tossers have responded, tell the group: **Sometimes things aren't what they appear to be. You might want to keep that in mind during the rest of this session.**

Non-Messy Option

Bring the game "Mousetrap," available at many toy stores. The game involves building an elaborate trap piece by piece. Play a round if you have time, or just have kids put the trap together and watch it work. Then discuss:

If you were the mouse, and you were sitting under the cage (the last part of the trap), and you saw someone turn the crank (the first step in the trap), would you be worried? (Probably not. The danger would seem pretty distant.)

When would you start to worry? When the boot kicked the bucket? When the ball rolled down the stairs? When the diver went into the tub?

(Answers may vary. But a mouse probably wouldn't sense danger until the trap was nearly sprung.)

Sometimes it's easy to get caught in a trap because we don't sense the danger coming. You might want to keep that in mind during the rest of this session.

2 HORNS, HOOVES, AND PITCHFORKS

Hand a blank sheet of paper to every student. Then explain: **We've probably all seen cartoon drawings or Hollywood versions of the devil. Being as artistic as you can, draw a picture showing what you think the devil might look like if he were to make an appearance. Be as creative as you want, but also try to be as accurate as you can based on what you understand to be true about the devil.**

Once kids are finished with their works of art, give them a chance to show what they came up with. Encourage them to point out any unique characteristics of their drawings and why those characteristics were included.

Then ask the group: **How were some of the drawings similar?** Chances are good that most, if not all the drawings will show the devil as a horned and hideous monster, a sinister man-like figure, or something equally unpleasant.

Now have a student look up and read II Corinthians 11:14, 15. Then ask the following questions:

How does this description of the devil fit with most of the pictures we drew? (It's a very different picture of how the devil might reveal himself to mankind. It's one that would probably look very attractive to most people, one that might even look almost right—almost, but not quite. In other words, the devil is in the deception business.)

Where do you think most people expect to find the devil doing his work? (A lot of people don't believe he exists. Those who do might expect to find him busy in hell; in places where demon-possession is reported, such as tribal regions; in satanic rituals, etc.)

Someone has said that the devil's most effective way to deceive people is to get them to believe he doesn't exist. Do you agree or disagree? Why?

Listen to replies. You may want to point out that if people don't believe in the devil, or at least don't believe he is working in "civilized" places like North America or Europe, they'll be easier targets for his deception and influence.

3 CATEGORICALLY SPEAKING

Hand out Student Sheet 11-A ("How Bad Is Bad?"). Give kids time to fill out the sheet individually. Then form small groups and have kids compare and discuss their choices with each other.

After kids have discussed their findings for a few minutes, bring them back together in the large group and ask the following questions:

How did you decide which activities went in a particular category? You may want to write responses on the board. This question helps students evaluate the thinking process they go through in drawing conclusions about spiritual matters.

Further, this question should help kids identify their *bases of authority*. That is, it should help them discover what sources they depend on to help them determine what they believe and why. Such authorities might include the Bible, their own powers of reasoning, some human authority figure in their lives (parent, teacher, youth leader, etc.), personal experience, what their peers say, etc.

Ask: **What discoveries did you make from the Scripture passages?**

Use the following information to supplement your discussion.

Deuteronomy 18:9-14—We must not be involved in human sacrifices, divination, sorcery, witchcraft, casting spells, or being a medium or spiritist who consults the dead. Anyone who does these things is detestable to the Lord; the Lord does not permit us to do these things.

Galatians 5:19-24—Idolatry and witchcraft—both associated with the occult—are included among a whole list of "the acts of the sinful nature." These are contrasted with "the fruit of the Spirit," including "love, joy, peace, patience, kindness, goodness, faithfulness, gentleness and self-control."

Revelation 20:11–21:8—This is the "Great White Throne Judgment," where the books are opened, the dead are judged, and the new heaven and earth are unveiled. See verse 8: "But the cowardly, the unbelieving, the vile, the murderers, the sexually immoral, those who practice magic arts, the idolaters and all liars—their place will be in the fiery lake of burning sulphur. This is the second death." Involvement in the occult ("magic arts") is not the only sin, but it is definitely on the list.

God clearly is not thrilled with this list of activities! Should they have any part in our lives, then?

If time allows, discuss how the activities listed on Student Sheet 11-A could relate to the verses just read.

Playing with Ouija boards—a form of divination, trying to find out "hidden knowledge" that God doesn't want us to seek.

Watching movies about ghosts—open to debate, but could lead a person to take lightly the idea of communicating with the dead.

Reading horoscopes—a form of divination.

Listening to heavy metal music—some, though not all, such music contains positive references to Satan and evil.

Learning to cast spells—this calls on the devil or demonic powers for the granting of wishes.

Holding a seance just for fun—seeks to communicate with the dead.

Watching movies about vampires and werewolves—open to debate, but these mythical creatures are closely associated with the occult and evil (note the movie vampire's reaction to a crucifix, for example).

Watching movies about demons or demon possession—these often make light of the demonic or make the devil seem more powerful than he really is; can also encourage an unhealthy fascination with the subject.

Being hypnotized—open to debate, but some have claimed that this opens a person to demonic influence.

Using tarot cards—a form of divination.

Trying drugs once or twice—some users of psychedelic drugs report what seemed like demonic contact during "bad trips."

Wearing crystals for good luck—attributing supernatural powers to crystals might amount to practicing "magic arts" or idolatry.

Watching TV shows that treat the devil as if he were funny—could lead a person not to take the devil, temptation, or hell seriously.

Having your fortune told—a form of divination.

Reading fantasy novels that have demon-like characters—could lead a person to think demons are fictional, or to develop an unhealthy interest in them.

Participating in role-playing games like "Dungeons and Dragons"—open to debate, but encourages interest in sorcery and casting spells.

Watching TV cartoons that include wizards or sorcerers—could encourage kids to think that sorcery is make-believe or even good.

Joining a satanic cult—obviously leads to worshiping the devil instead of the one true God; in some cases has led members to sexual immorality, murder, and other sins.

4 TRUE STORIES

Hand out Student Sheet 11-B ("The Ouija Board"). Have kids read this true story to themselves, or take turns reading it aloud. Then discuss:

Why was Lisa interested in the Ouija board? (Her friends were using it; it seemed to have special powers and give special knowledge to those who used it.)

Why did the board seem harmless at first? (Her friends had used it; it could be bought along with other games at the store; it claimed to be good, not evil, and even to speak on behalf of Jesus.)

Did being involved in the occult bring her what she expected? (No; the voice behind the board was a liar seeking to make her a slave.)

How could Lisa and her family have avoided the trouble they got into? (By staying away from the board; by being better informed on what the Bible says about the occult.)

When should Lisa have said no to using the board? (There were many opportunities to get rid of the board, but it would have been best to say no the first time her friends encouraged her to try it.)

How do you think Lisa and her family would answer the question, "What's so bad about playing around with the occult?"

5 WHAT DOES EVIL SMELL LIKE?

If you have time, tell the following story.

The Poas Volcano is a big attraction in Costa Rica. Every year thousands of tourists make the long, bumpy drive up the mountainside to look down into the mouth of a live volcano.

All around the volcano are large signs that say, DANGER: TOXIC FUMES. DO NOT GO BEYOND DESIGNATED VIEWING AREA. The signs are there because the most deadly fumes given off by volcanoes are odorless. Before you could smell any danger, it would be too late.

Some curious tourists wanted to get a better look at the mouth of the volcano than the "designated viewing area" would allow. So they decided to jump the rail and walk down for a closer look. So far, several have died.

Then discuss the following question:

How is that volcano like the occult?

(Our curiosity about evil may seem quite harmless, but can result in deadly consequences, killing us—spiritually or even physically—before we realize what's happened.)

End the session today by having kids read Ephesians 6:10-18, one verse per student, as a kind of last word on the topic. Then have kids silently reflect on and pray about how the passage has spoken to them. After a minute or two, dismiss.

How Bad Is Bad?

Place a check mark in the column that you think best describes each activity. Then look up the verses at the bottom and write down any discoveries that might help you figure out where to place some of the questionable activities.

	Definitely evil and dangerous	Unsure	Definitely not evil or dangerous
Playing with Ouija boards			
Watching movies about ghosts			
Reading horoscopes			
Listening to heavy metal music			
Learning to cast spells			
Holding a seance just for fun			
Watching movies about vampires and werewolves			
Watching movies about demons or demon possession			
Being hypnotized			
Using tarot cards			
Trying drugs once or twice			
Wearing crystals for good luck			
Watching TV shows that treat the devil as if he were funny			
Having your fortune told			
Reading fantasy novels that have demon-like characters			
Participating in role-playing games like "Dungeons and Dragons"			
Watching TV cartoons that include wizards or sorcerers			
Joining a satanic cult			

Deuteronomy 18:9-14:

Galatians 5:19-24:

Revelation 20:11—21:8:

The Ouija Board

(A Ouija board is a board printed with the alphabet and other symbols. The user, trying to receive "supernatural" messages, holds a pointer against the board. The pointer moves, spelling out words and sentences.)

The following is based on a true story; names have been changed.

One night Lisa was invited to join friends who gathered regularly to use a Ouija board. The rec room felt cold as she watched the board spell out messages in answer to her friends' questions.

"Come on," they urged. "Sit in this time. Try it yourself."

Lisa knew her friends claimed they'd contacted spirits who spoke through the Ouija board. Was it true? Or were her friends just making the pointer move? Scared but fascinated, she sat down—and discovered that the pointer really seemed to spell out messages without being pushed.

Not long after that night, Lisa lost contact with those friends when her family moved away. But a year later she met a woman who said she'd used a Ouija board to contact relatives who had died. Lisa's curiosity grew, and this time she bought a board of her own.

That night, the members of Lisa's family began to use the board, asking it questions—and getting answers. They would begin by asking a question they'd been told to ask for their "protection": "Do you come in the white light of the Lord?"

The board would spell out, "Yes."

Night after night the family would stay up late with the board. Sometimes Lisa would pause to enter an answer in her diary.

About the time Lisa brought the board home, a stray cat showed up at her door. The family adopted it. Each time the board was played, the cat would sit nearby, watching. One night the board spelled out a chilling message: "The cat has a spirit."

But Lisa and her family kept using the board, thinking it was just a game—like Monopoly or checkers.

Then one night the board spelled out, "I have a pleasant surprise. Someone wants to speak with you."

"Do you come in the white light of the Lord?" asked the family member who was using the board.

"Yes," came the reply. "I am Jesus, the Son of God."

Lisa's family believed it. From then on they thought the board's answers were from Jesus. When they would ask, "Who is on the board?" the reply would be, "I am the Lord."

Five months after Lisa got the board, a neighbor stopped in and saw the family using it. She was shocked. "What you're doing is dangerous," the neighbor said. "It is against what the Bible says."

Later the neighbor brought over a pamphlet about the occult. It quoted

Deuteronomy 18:10, 11 and said that Ouija boards were a way of communicating with demons.

Lisa was scared. Had the devil been impersonating Jesus? That night she and her family asked the board, "What do you want from us?"

"Your souls," it said.

The family member using the board said, "You're not getting that." But the board spelled out, "Ha, ha."

That was it. Lisa and her family grabbed the board and threw it into the fireplace, where it burned to ashes.

Soon the cat they'd adopted—the one the board said had a spirit—became very ill and had to be destroyed.

Lisa and her family now share their story with others, to warn them. They say that Satan is real, not a superstitious idea. They want others to know that Jesus is revealed through the Bible—not through Ouija boards.

—Marion Duckworth
© 1976

Session 12

Today's beer commercials are amusing, entertaining, and sometimes downright appealing. Big bucks are spent to make the suds look irresistible, and it shows.

The messages are clear: "You can't be cool without alcohol." "You won't get the guy or the girl without drinking." "You can't have any fun without a brew." "You won't have any friends if you don't chug a few." Kids are buying it—in every sense of the word.

Your kids need a chance to think through where they're getting their information about drinking and where to get the rest of the story. That's what this session is about.

Drinking alcohol is a controversial issue in many churches, and not all the issues are crystal clear. As you lead this session, remember that your goal is to help kids develop their *own* convictions—based as much on scriptural principles as possible. If kids take "ownership" of any principles they learn today, you will have given them a gift that keeps on giving.

IS THERE ANYTHING WRONG WITH DRINKING?

Specific Aims

• To help kids understand that, while not all drinking is condemned in the Bible, drunkenness is; to help kids compare the positive aspects of drinking (of which there are few) with the negative aspects (of which there are many); and to encourage kids to see Scripture, not peer pressure, as the most credible source of answers to this question.

Scriptural Support

• Proverbs 20:1; 23:29-35
• Romans 13:1, 2, 13, 14; 14:13-21
• I Corinthians 6:12; 10:23–11:1
• Ephesians 5:18
• I Thessalonians 5:4-8
• I Peter 4:1-7

Special Preparation

• Bibles
• Copies of Student Sheet 12-A ("I.Q. Test")
• Copies of Student Sheet 12-B ("Alcohol and Its Effects")
• Copies of Student Sheet 12-C ("True Stories")
• Pencils
• Chalkboard and chalk or newsprint and marker
• Watch or stopwatch

1 IF ALL ELSE FAILS . . .

Hand out Student Sheet 12-A ("I.Q. Test"). As you pass out the sheets, give the following instructions very clearly: **Read and follow the directions at the top of the page before beginning. The object of the game is to finish as quickly as possible.** Look at your watch for effect. Then say: **Go.**

Wait until all students finish or until they figure out that they were supposed to read all the directions and only follow #8.

Then ask: **What's the moral of the story?**

What went wrong for the people who actually went through the activities? (They didn't follow the directions at the top carefully enough; it says to read all the directions first and then follow them.)

Life tends to run more smoothly when we're careful to follow the directions. Many good things, even gifts from God, can become worthless if not destructive when not used according to their directions.

Where do people get their directions for living? Think of as many sources of direction as you can. (The Bible, parents, teachers, friends, church, TV, coaches, the government, labels on products, street signs, maps, experts, etc.)

What directions are the sources we just mentioned giving us when it comes to drinking alcoholic beverages? Give kids a chance to brainstorm ideas. You may want to write some on the board.

2 . . . READ THE DIRECTIONS

Say: **The Bible is certainly not the only source we have for getting directions, but it's the only source that claims to have God's directions for us. Before we look at it, tell me in one or two sentences: What do you think the Bible says about drinking?**

Let kids reply. Some may think it prohibits all drinking of alcohol; others may think some drinking is allowed; others may not know either way.

Let's check out what the Bible has to say about drinking.

Form three small groups. Have each look up one of the following sets of verses and determine what it says about drinking.

Group 1—I Corinthians 6:12; 10:23–11:1; Romans 14:13-21

Group 2—Proverbs 20:1; 23:29-35; I Peter 4:1-7

Group 3—I Thessalonians 5:4-8; Ephesians 5:18; Romans 13:1, 2, 13, 14

Allow several minutes for groups to work on their assignments. Then discuss their responses, writing key phrases on the board (save these notes for later). Use the following information as necessary.

Group 1—It may be permissible to drink, but not wise or beneficial; it should never cause weaker brothers to stumble.

Group 2—To be drunk is to be stupid; alcohol is dangerous stuff; being drunk isn't cool, but people may hassle you for not drinking.

Group 3—If the law says not to drink (and it does, if you're underage), you are to obey; don't get drunk; be alert, self-controlled, and filled with the Spirit.

Is that pretty much what you expected the Bible to say?

How would you summarize these teachings in a sentence or two?

3 SCIENCE SPEAKS

You may be thinking, "Sure, that's what the Bible says. But the Bible's always against fun stuff. The rest of the world thinks drinking is fine."

Does it? Let's take scientific evidence, for instance. What are the physical effects of alcohol on your body?

Let kids make suggestions. Then pass out Student Sheet 12-B ("Alcohol and Its Effects"). Let kids read this silently, or take turns reading it aloud.

Then say: **Please underline on this sheet all the positive effects that alcohol has on the body.**

Give kids a moment to look for these. Some may underline "The first drink of alcohol acts as a stimulant . . ." Even this is debatable as a positive effect, though.

Now circle all the negative effects.

(It alters mood; can be addictive; depresses parts of the brain; causes unsteady walking and slurred speech; judgment and coordination are affected; the individual may sleep, laugh or cry uncontrollably, or become antagonistic; at increased alcohol levels the person falls into a stupor, lapses into a coma, or even dies; with prolonged use more is required to produce a "high"; affects vision, muscular control, memory, and performance; causes liver damage and other kinds of physical deterioration.)

If you were a parent, would you want your teenager to be affected by alcohol in these ways? Why or why not?

4 VOICES OF EXPERIENCE

There's another way to get directions in life. It's listening to people who have "been there"—in this case, kids who have tried drinking. Here are the true stories of three kids like that.

Form the three small groups again. Pass out copies of Student Sheet 12-C ("True Stories"). Assign a story to each group. Groups should read their stories and answer the following questions:

Why did this person start drinking?

What was the result?

After giving kids a couple of minutes to come up with answers, regather the whole group and share results. As needed, use the following information.

LuAnn—She started drinking because she didn't like herself. She felt drinking was the only way to fit in and keep her boyfriend. The result was that she became addicted and went on to using other drugs.

Gordon—He started drinking as part of his rebellion. Maybe he was rebelling against the "good boy" image he had. The result was that he quit going to church and associating with other Christians, and later he felt he had to keep his drinking a secret from them.

Dan—He started drinking out of curiosity, then to dull the pain he felt over his mom's death and his dad's remarriage. The result was that he led a double life, got ulcers, and eventually went on to drugs that were even more dangerous.

In your opinion, why do kids in general start drinking? Are their reasons better than those of LuAnn, Gordon, and Dan?

Do you think these three kids should have known what would happen when they started drinking? Why or why not?

If a beer company asked these three people to be in a beer commercial on TV tomorrow, what do you think they would say?

5 PLAN AHEAD

Keep kids in the three small groups. Call their attention to the phrases you wrote on the board as a result of the Bible study in Step 2.

I'm going to throw out some questions about drinking that you may get from other kids. Using the Bible verses your group looked up, plus any other verses you want to use, plus your own opinion, tell me how you could answer them.

(NOTE: Allow kids to express opinions that differ with the conclusions you've reached, or with those that seem to be taught in the Bible passages. But challenge them to show why their opinions are consistent with or superior to the Bible's directions.)

Question 1: "Hey, aren't you going to have some? There's nothing wrong with drinking if you don't get drunk, is there?"

Give groups a minute to come up with replies. Here are some thoughts to use if desired:

While the Bible does not literally say, "Having a drink is sin," it does seem to indicate that alcohol can be a dangerous substance (Proverbs 20:1). Also take note of I Corinthians 6:12 and I Corinthians 10:23. Not all permissible things are beneficial or constructive, and nothing—no matter how permissible it is—should master us. Furthermore, underage drinking is against the law, and Christians are to obey the law.

(NOTE: If kids bring up the fact that Jesus turned water into wine, you may want to note that there's disagreement over whether it was fermented. Even if it was, alcohol played a different role in His culture than in ours—as a basic beverage that could be safer to drink than water. Some Christians today have decided to abstain from alcohol because alcohol addiction is such a problem in our culture.)

Question 2: "Loosen up. What's wrong with getting a little 'buzzed' now and then just for fun?"

Drunkenness is clearly forbidden in Scripture (Ephesians 5:18; Romans

13:13, 14). Many an argument has been raised concerning where to draw the line between "still sober" and "drunk." Some suggested verses to consider in drawing conclusions here are I Thessalonians 5:6-8 and I Peter 4:7. If we have lost any degree of self-control or alertness, we have probably gone too far—and even a little alcohol can affect us in those ways. The command to obey the laws about underage drinking apply here, too.

Question 3: "All our friends drink. What are we supposed to do? If we don't drink they'll think we're losers."

It's very possible that some friends will think we're strange if we choose not to get drunk or at least drink with them. This may be part of the cost we must pay if we're going to follow Jesus (I Peter 4:1-5).

While the kinds of friends we choose is a session for another day, you may want to encourage kids who are interested to check out I Corinthians 15:33; Proverbs 13:20; Proverbs 17:17; and Proverbs 18:24.

You may want to close this session by letting kids know you are available to them if they need to talk further about drinking. Kids face tremendous peer pressure in this area—maybe even from others in your group—and a one-on-one setting may encourage some to be a lot more open than they might be in the meeting.

I.Q. TEST

Time: _____

Read all the directions and then follow them as *quickly* as you can. Once you finish, record the time at the top of your handout. Then sit quietly until the rest of the group has had a chance to finish.

1. Add the following numbers: 268, 459, 70, 1325, 654. Then subtract that number from 123,456. Then multiply it by 7. Finally divide that number by 3. Write your answer here: _____.

2. Compose a sentence in which every letter in the alphabet is used. It can be as long or short as you choose.

3. Recite your name aloud. Then reverse the letters, and recite your name backwards aloud. Example, if your name was John Doe, you would say "John Doe," then "eoD nhoJ" (sounds like ee-odd, nawj).

4. Say the word, "antidisestablishmentarianism" aloud three times as fast as you can.

5. Say one word or phrase aloud in every language you know, including English. After you have done this, write in the blank the number of languages you spoke: _____.

6. Recite aloud one song title that you know from each of the following decades: the 90s, 80s, 70s, and 60s.

7. Draw a picture of an object so that it appears to be three-dimensional. You can be as simple or elaborate as you wish.

8. Do not follow any of the instructions except this one. This is the only instruction you are to follow. Just sit quietly and wait for the rest of the class to finish.

9. Stand up and do 10 jumping jacks while yelling, "I can fly! I can fly!"

10. Sing the first verse of "Row, Row, Row Your Boat" as loudly as possible.

ALCOHOL AND ITS EFFECTS

Because the manufacture, sale, and consumption of beverage alcohol is legal and socially acceptable, it is not always thought of as a drug. But that's exactly what it is, because it contains ethyl alcohol or ethanol, a mood-altering substance.

Beer and wine are no less harmful than whiskey. A 4.5 percent, sixteen-ounce can of beer, a five-ounce glass of wine, and a one-and-a-half-ounce shot glass of hundred-proof whiskey each contain about three-fourths ounce of alcohol. So individuals who say, "I can't be (or become) addicted because I only drink beer (or wine)" are fooling themselves. (Specific figures depend on the alcohol content of each beverage.)

The first drink of alcohol acts as a stimulant, but when more is consumed, the alcohol depresses parts of the brain. As a result, the drinker may weave when he or she walks and slur his or her speech. Judgment and coordination are affected. As more is consumed, the individual may sleep, laugh or cry uncontrollably, or become antagonistic.

When the drinker's blood alcohol level rises even more, he or she falls into a stupor. If the level reaches .4 or .5 percent, the person lapses into a coma. Still higher levels can suppress breathing and heartbeat and cause death.

The more alcohol an individual uses over a period of time, the greater his or her tolerance to it will be and the more he or she will require to produce the same result. Vision, muscular control, memory loss and performance, liver damage, and other evidences of physical deterioration are only some of the long-term effects.

—Adapted from *Substance Abuse* by William Davis, Patricia Myers, and Marion Duckworth (David C. Cook)

True Stories

LuAnn

LuAnn was in church regularly. She made the effort even though no one else in her family attended.

As a teenager, she'd been a leader in her youth group for a couple of years when a guy caught her eye. He was also a member of the youth group, but he used alcohol. "To be his girlfriend," LuAnn recalls, "I did what he and his crowd did. That meant getting drunk every weekend and sometimes more often. I had low self-esteem and thought I was homely, and here was this male attention with tenderness and touching—things that were foreign to me. That pretty much took my focus off the Lord."

By the time LuAnn was sixteen, she and her boyfriend broke up. Later she met and married a rock musician. In addition to alcohol, she began smoking pot and using hallucinogens like LSD and mescaline. The next few years were a roller coaster of addictive behavior.

Gordon

Gordon's addiction began in high school, too. Raised in a stable Christian home, he attended church regularly and acquired a lapel full of perfect attendance pins. But unlike his siblings, Gordon was a rebel: "As a teenager, I got drunk a couple of weekends a month and drank even more when I got out of high school."

He says now that he came to know Jesus Christ as a teenager, but dropped out of church during those years. He sometimes attended other churches as an adult when he was trying to remain clean and sober, but that never lasted long. Like LuAnn, he was secretive about his addiction, and no one in pulpit or pew knew.

Dan

The first time Dan got drunk, he was at home in the parsonage basement. Thirteen years old and the son of a minister, he and his stepbrother found some lemon extract and had a contest to see who could drink the most at one time. They finished off the seemingly-innocent little bottle, which was ninety-six percent alcohol.

Getting drunk seemed like a positive experience at the time, recalls Dan. It desensitized him to the confusion tearing at him over the death of his mother the year before, and it dulled his anger at his father's subsequent remarriage.

"Through high school, I drank whatever I could get." But Dan's double life—one as the obedient preacher's kid who was a youth group faithful and the other as the mainstay in the party crowd that drank to get intoxicated—had a high price. By the time he was sixteen, Dan required treatment for ulcers that had developed partly from worrying that his drinking would be found out. He also suffered frequent headaches.

During high school, Dan started using all kinds of drugs. By the time he was a senior, he was experimenting with heroin and now considers himself addicted to drugs during those years.

—Adapted from *Substance Abuse* by William Davis, Patricia Myers, and Marion Duckworth (David C. Cook)

Session 13

If ever there's been an issue that set mother against daughter and son against father, it's rock music.

It's been that way in the church, too. Not long ago, one well-known Christian stated publicly that rock—both Christian and secular—has an evil influence on young people. At least 5,000 fans of contemporary Christian music responded by writing letters about how that kind of music has been spiritually helpful to them.

This session will not end the debate. But it will get your kids expressing their feelings about their music. It will also get them thinking about their own Bible-based answers to the question of whether rock is OK. That's no small task; as veteran youth leader Dave Veerman writes, "[Rock] is an intellectual issue, but most kids feel deeply about their music and can get pretty worked up about it."

Here's an opportunity to help kids cool down for a while and take a more objective look at what they've been putting in their ears.

Is Rock Music OK?

Specific Aims
• To help kids objectively examine rock music; and to help them understand that everything in their lives should glorify God—including the music they listen to.

Scriptural Support
• Proverbs 13:20
• Mark 12:28-31
• I Corinthians 10:31–11:1; 15:33, 34
• Galatians 5:16-25
• Philippians 1:27, 28; 4:8

Special Preparation
• Bibles
• Copies of Student Sheet 13-A ("The Acid Test")
• Copies of Student Sheet 13-B ("Conversation on a Plane")
• Copies of Student Sheet 13-C ("Rock around the Clock")
• Pencils
• Chalkboard and chalk or newsprint and marker
• Paper
• AM-FM radio
• Partial roll of butcher paper or shelf paper
• Variety of colored markers

1 RIDING THE FM DIAL

Bring an AM-FM radio. Before the meeting starts, get early arrivals to help you draw on butcher paper or shelf paper a representation of the FM dial. This will probably look like a long rectangle with numbered marks running across the top. Tape or otherwise fasten the paper to the wall.

When the group arrives, hand out a variety of colored markers.

We're going to "ride the FM dial" today. As we listen to each station for a few seconds, decide what color each kind of music reminds you of. When we come to a station that reminds you of the color(s) you're holding, come up to the chart and color in that part of the dial. If more than one person comes up at the same time, squeeze your colors next to each other on the chart.

Choose a volunteer to be the radio "tuner" who will work his or her way across the FM dial, tuning in to each station that is playing music. Have him or her start on one end of the FM dial and tune slowly to the other end, pausing to let kids come up and color the chart.

When the "dial" is complete, you'll probably see a wide variety of colors—even for the same kind of music. Discuss:

Why did you match these colors with these kinds of music as you did?

Why didn't we all pick the same colors for the same music? (We associate colors and music with different emotions; we have different reactions to music, and different tastes.)

Some people have pretty strong reactions to music. And they feel that their favorite kinds of music are the best. This can lead to some major arguments.

2 WE'RE NUMBER ONE

Have kids form groups according to their favorite styles of music. For instance, if you have a few kids whose favorite style of music is "head-banging" rock, group them together. If you have some whose favorite style is classical music, group them together.

Say: **Your job as a group is to declare why you think your favorite music style is the "best" style. You'll have one minute to present your case to the rest of the groups, so try to be as convincing as possible. Your goal is to persuade the others that they should switch to your style, since it is clearly the "best" style of music.**

Give groups a few minutes to come up with their presentations. Then give each group a minute to present its reasons to the rest. (Adjust the time and the number of groups so as to spend a total of about 10 minutes on this activity.)

After all the groups have presented their reasons, bring the whole group back together.

Ask: **Who do you think had the most persuasive case? Why?**

Do you think their arguments apply to every song in their style? Why or why not?

3 RATE THE RECORDINGS

For the rest of this session, let's talk specifically about one kind of music: rock. **What do you think is the best rock song of last year?**

Of this year?

What was the worst rock song of last year?

This year?

There will be plenty of disagreements about these, but that's fine. Avoid getting bogged down in a debate.

How did you decide which songs were best and which were worst? ("The music sounds great [or stinks]"; "The group that sings the song is excellent [or reeks]"; "All my friends [none of my friends] like the song," etc.)

If you wanted to evaluate whether or not a song was worth listening to, what questions do you think you should ask about it to help you decide?

Hand out copies of Student Sheet 13-A ("The Acid Test"). Give kids a few minutes to respond by themselves. Then discuss the sheet as a group.

Ask kids which questions they felt were most important and which were least important. You may want to add any that you feel are crucial if kids fail to mention them.

Some of the more important issues to consider (you or your church may want to add others) are:

1. The lyrics of the song. See Philippians 4:8 for the kinds of input God wants us to have. Some of the questions that address the lyrics are:

What kinds of attitudes does the song promote?

In what directions do the words encourage my mind to go?

What kinds of decisions do the lyrics encourage me to make?

2. The effect of the music on the listener's emotional state. Different kinds of music have different kinds of impact on the emotions of the listener. A ballad might encourage sentimental reflection; an upbeat tune might encourage excitement, etc. Helpful questions might include:

Does the song's musical style contribute to my loving God and others or does it distract me from doing so? (See Mark 12:28-31.)

Does the song's musical style seem to give me an emotional lift or does it tend to drag me down emotionally?

3. The lifestyle of the musician or group. This issue is often raised in discussions about rock music. It should be noted, however, that few (if any) styles of music stand up under scrutiny in this category, either. Even classical music has had its share of scandalous composers and musicians. While this should not be used as an excuse by those who listen to an immoral rock group or singer, it would be hypocritical to apply a "lifestyle" standard to rock music but not to other forms of music. Having said that, some helpful questions might include:

Does the musician or group have a sense of social responsibility (compassion toward the poor and oppressed) that I want to imitate?

Does the musician or group model the kind of personal morality that I want to imitate? (See Proverbs 13:20; I Corinthians 15:33, 34.)

As you discuss the scriptural principles at the bottom of the handout, use the following information as a guide:

I Corinthians 10:31–11:1

Possible questions include:

As far as I can tell, does listening to this song glorify God in any way?

What kind of example does my listening set for other Christians?

Galatians 5:16-25

Possible questions include:

Which kind of fruit does the song encourage me to produce: the acts of the sinful nature or the fruit of the Spirit?

Does the song make it easier or more difficult for me to "crucify the sinful nature" and keep in step with the Spirit?

Philippians 1:27, 28

Possible questions include:

Does the song promote conduct that is worthy of the Gospel of Christ?

Am I so "into" the musician(s) that I can't bring myself to take a stand against him, her, or them?

4 AFTEREFFECTS

Have two volunteers read aloud Student Sheet 13-B ("Conversation on a Plane") playing the parts of Al Menconi and the young man. Then discuss:

What is Al's answer to people who say that song lyrics don't affect them?

(If other forms of communication influence us and teach us things, why not music and lyrics?)

Does Al's reasoning make sense to you?

Let kids reply or just think about it. To wrap up the session, hand out Student Sheet 13-C ("Rock around the Clock") for kids to take with them.

This week I hope you'll think through and answer each of the questions on these sheets. Since this is for your personal application, we won't be discussing our answers in the group. Your job is to apply what you decide.

THE ACID TEST

Rate the following questions on a scale of 1 (totally important) to 5 (totally unimportant) in terms of how helpful and appropriate you think they are in deciding whether a song is worth listening to.

___ Do I like the style of music in the song?

___ What kinds of attitudes does the song promote?

___ What do my friends think about this song?

___ How do my pets respond to this song?

___ Does the musician or group have a sense of social responsibility (compassion toward the poor and oppressed) I want to imitate?

___ Does the musician or group have the kind of personal hygiene I want to imitate?

___ In what directions do the words encourage my mind to go?

___ Does the musician singing the song make any stops on tour in cities that I would consider repulsive and never visit myself?

___ What kinds of decisions do the lyrics encourage me to make?

___ Are the outfits of the musicians appropriate for Sunday morning worship service?

___ Does the song's musical style contribute to my loving God and others or does it distract me from doing so?

___ Does the musician or group model the kind of personal morality that I want to imitate?

___ Does the name of the musician or group start with the same letter as my middle name?

___ Does the song's musical style seem to give me an emotional lift or does it tend to drag me down emotionally?

___ Does the artwork on the CD or cassette case clash with my other CDs or cassettes?

What other questions do you think the following verses might give you to help you decide?

I Corinthians 10:31–11:1 _____

_____

Galatians 5:16-25 _____

_____

Philippians 1:27, 28 _____

_____

CONVERSATION ON A PLANE

The following conversation took place between Al Menconi, a Christian who speaks and writes about rock music, and a young man he met on a plane. The conversation is adapted from *Today's Music: A Window to Your Child's Soul* by Al Menconi with Dave Hart (David C. Cook).

YOUNG MAN: I like heavy metal, but it doesn't affect me.

AL: Oh, really? How do you know it doesn't?

YOUNG MAN: Well, I enjoy listening to it, but I'm not a Satanist or anything like that.

AL: Ozzy [Osbourne] doesn't claim to be a Satanist either. It's just a gimmick to him. So why would you think you would become a Satanist if you listened to Ozzy's music?

YOUNG MAN: I just meant that his music doesn't make me kill small animals or beat up my little brother, or anything.

AL: Why do you listen to it?

YOUNG MAN: Because it sounds so good.

AL: Tell me, do your teachers ever show movies in class?

YOUNG MAN: Sure, sometimes.

AL: Do they use videos, television, slides, and audiotapes?

YOUNG MAN: Yeah, they do.

AL: Do you know why?

YOUNG MAN: It's more interesting, I know that.

AL: Those things are also good teaching tools. Now think. When you take that same tool out of your classroom and put it in your home, what do you call it?

YOUNG MAN: I guess it's TV.

AL: How about MTV?

YOUNG MAN: Yeah, I see what you're saying.

AL: So if it's instruction in the classroom, isn't it still instruction in the home? You're learning the values of your favorite groups, whether you realize it or not.

Rock around the Clock

Think through and answer each of the following questions. Since this is for your personal application, your answers will not be discussed in the group. Try to be as honest and accurate as you can.

Filling up the Hours
Starting from the 12, fill in the clock (like a pie chart) with the number of hours a day you spend listening to rock music.

Racking up the Bucks
Starting at zero, fill in the coin (like a pie chart) to show the number of dollars you spend in an average month to listen to rock music, including CDs, tapes, concerts, T-shirts, etc.

Sizing up the Songs

Fill in between the headphones three messages that you hear most often when listening to the kind of rock music that you listen to.

Making up My Mind

Which one or more of the following suggestions do you think would help you move toward a better balance in life when it comes to rock music?

__ I won't listen to rock music at all.
__ I will listen to rock music no more than __ hours a week.
__ I will try to spend as much time reading my Bible and other Christian books as I do listening to rock music.
__ I will only listen to Christian rock music.
__ I will change the station when songs come on that I believe are not pleasing to God or that I think violate my Christian standards.
__ Here's my own idea: _____

Would you be willing to try to apply at least one of the statements that you checked above? You might be suprised at the results.

Chances are that you don't hear a lot of profanity and vulgar language during your youth group meetings. But follow your kids to their schools, athletic fields, malls, and fast food restaurants and you'll hear a different story.

Even if your own young people are watching their language, they're surrounded by others who aren't. From friends, movies, TV, music, and some parents, kids today hear more "swearing" than many truck drivers used to hear. Using forbidden four-letter words became a symbol of rebellion and liberation a few decades ago, and that legacy will be with us for a long time.

Add to this input the surging emotional turbulence most adolescents feel, and you've got plenty of reasons to expect a lot of cursing, vulgarity, and blasphemy. Your mission in this session is to give your kids some good reasons not to accept "swearing" as standard conversational procedure.

EVERYONE SWEARS, SO WHY CAN'T I?

Specific Aims

• To help kids recognize that it's important to honor God with our speech, even if the people around us don't.

Scriptural Support

• Exodus 20:7
• Matthew 5:22; 10:28; 12:33-36
• Romans 14:13-15, 19
• Ephesians 5:3, 4
• James 3:9-11
• I John 2:9, 10

Special Preparation

• Bibles
• Three copies of Student Sheet 14-A ("What's Wrong with This Picture?")
• Copies of Student Sheet 14-B ("What's the Big Deal?")
• Copies of Student Sheet 14-C ("Programming Guide")
• Pens
• A couple of rolls of toilet paper
• Rest room

1 CENSORED SCENE

Give three volunteers, preferably two guys and a girl, copies of the skit on Student Sheet 14-A ("What's Wrong with This Picture?"). Let them read it to themselves while you introduce the skit.

We're about to see a scene from an upcoming major motion picture. The picture is *Killhard Die Big II*. The characters are Jack Hammer, tough police detective; Billy Scar, drug dealer; and Linda Lipgloss, Jack's girlfriend. The scene takes place in a dark alley.

Have your actors perform the skit, having fun with it. After they're done, thank them and lead the group in applause. Then discuss:

Did anything strike you as strange about this scene? (For one thing, the characters used a lot of flowery words—instead of the strong language you'd expect to hear in a movie.)

Do you think we should expect to hear a lot of strong language or swearing in movies and TV?

In real life?

Without listing the actual words, what types of words do you think of as strong language or swearing? (Curses, vulgar sexual or "bathroom" terms, using God's name in vain, etc.)

How do you feel when you hear people swearing in movies or on TV? In real life?

Do you think people swear more or less than they did when your parents were kids? Why or why not?

How do you think God feels about swearing?

2 TOILET TALK

Pass around pens and a roll of toilet paper (make sure you bring enough for each person to take several sheets) and say: **Tear from the roll the number of sheets of toilet paper that you think represents the average number of times a day that you find yourself tempted to swear. But don't take more than ten sheets, or we might run out!**

Once everyone has had a chance to tear off sheets, say: **Now, take your first sheet of toilet paper and write on it one situation that you face regularly in which you struggle with swearing or at least wanting to swear. Do this for each sheet of toilet paper that you took from the roll.**

If the group struggles to think of examples, you might suggest some: "When I get into an argument with my brother"; "When I mess up during basketball practice"; "When so-and-so knocks my tray out of my hands in the school cafeteria"; "When I bump my head getting into the car," etc. Once kids have had a chance to write something on each of their sheets of toilet paper, move on to the next activity.

3 WHAT'S THE BIG DEAL?

Form at least four small groups if possible. Pass out copies of Student Sheet 14-B ("What's the Big Deal?").

What's the big deal about swearing? Let's look at some real-life-type situations.

Assign at least one of the situations to each group or individual. Kids should read their situations, look up the corresponding Bible passages on the sheet, and discuss Bible-based replies to the question, "What's the big deal?"

After a few minutes, regather the whole group. Have small groups summarize their situations, their passages, and their replies. As needed, supplement their comments with the following information.

1. Misusing God's name shows that you don't take Him seriously enough (Exodus 20:7). It's pretty easy to see that blasphemy (insulting or being irreverent toward God) is wrong. But using His name without meaning (as in saying "Oh, God" or "Jesus" when you're just expressing disgust) is using it in vain, too.

2. Using words like "hell" without meaning them shows that you don't take those ideas seriously enough (Matthew 10:28; 12:36). To "damn" someone is serious business. Using these terms as throwaway words encourages people to think of hell as just a word, not a real place.

3. "Cussing people out" shows that you don't love them (Matthew 5:22; James 3:9-11; I John 2:9, 10). How can you curse someone and love that person at the same time? Even if no one (except God) hears you, your attitude of hate is still there.

4. Using vulgar language shows that you don't care whether you offend the people around you (Ephesians 5:3, 4; Romans 14:13-15, 19). It's true that language changes, and some words that used to be taboo are seen as innocent now. (For example, in Victorian times it was considered improper to speak of a woman's "leg"; the word "limb" was to be substituted.) But some words, even if they don't insult God or curse others, are still very offensive to many people. A Christian is to avoid offending others in order to keep peace and spread the Good News. Does that mean it's OK to be vulgar if you're surrounded by vulgar people? Not according to Ephesians 5:3, 4.

4 CHECKING THE PROGRAMMING

You've probably heard the computer programming expression, "Garbage in—garbage out." So far we've looked at the language that comes out of us. Now let's take a look at what goes in.

Hand out copies of Student Sheet 14-C ("Programming Guide"). Give kids time to think through Matthew 12:33-35, the three stages discussed, and their application.

In one sentence, what do you think is the message of this sheet?

("What goes in must come out"; "What goes into your mind gets stored in your heart, and what gets stored in your heart comes out of your mouth sooner or later"; "If you want to watch what you say, watch what you hear," etc.)

If any volunteers are willing, let them tell what they crossed out and circled on the sheet and why.

5 TOILET TALK II

Take the sheets of toilet paper you wrote on earlier in the meeting. Choose one of them and read the situation to yourself. Think of how you'll face that if it happens this week. If you are willing to commit yourself in the presence of the rest of the group to not swearing in that situation, put that sheet of toilet paper here on the floor.

Once kids have piled their paper on the floor, gather up the sheets and march the group to the nearest rest room. With as much dramatic effect as you can muster, drop the sheets of toilet paper into a toilet and flush them into oblivion. (To avoid clogging up the toilet, you might want to take a couple of flushes to flush all the sheets down—better safe than soggy.)

Now take the rest of your sheets with you. Next time you face one of those situations without swearing, flush those sheets, too.

As you dismiss group members, encourage them to remember their applications from the bottom of the "Programming Guide" as well.

WHAT'S WRONG WITH THIS PICTURE? 14-A

Scene One from the movie, *Killhard Die Big II.*

Characters: Jack Hammer, tough police detective; Billy Scar, drug dealer; Linda Lipgloss, Jack's girlfriend

Place: A dark alley

HAMMER: So, Billy, you nasty individual. You thought you could get a ton of illegal drugs past me, eh? You little misguided fellow. I'd like to take this gun and use it in some way.

BILLY: Hammer, you police officer. Why don't you go spend your time in a way which does not bother me?

HAMMER: You make me want to shake my head. You and your kind are a bunch of confused persons.

BILLY: Is that correct? Maybe you'll change your mind when I use this knife I've been hiding in my boot.

HAMMER: Oh, my goodness gracious!

LINDA: It's OK, Hammer. I've got you covered.

HAMMER: Linda! What in cornflakes are you doing here?

LINDA: I heard this little law-breaking person was giving you trouble.

BILLY: You silly female individual. I ought to object to your presence here.

HAMMER: Please stop talking, Billy. You'll have plenty of time for that where you're going.

BILLY: Indeed? And where would that be?

HAMMER: To an incarceration facility.

LINDA: Oh, Hammer. I enjoy it when you use such a vocabulary. It makes me want to hold hands.

HAMMER: No time for that now, Linda. I have to take this little rebellious person downtown.

BILLY: What's the charge, you law fellow?

HAMMER: Using bad language. You said the word "silly."

BILLY: Oh, pancakes!

HAMMER: Watch your mouth, Billy. There's a lady present.

BILLY: Sorry.

What's the Big Deal?

1. Carl watches a lot of TV, especially comedies. Many of the characters in these shows say things like, "Oh, God!" when they're surprised or disgusted. Carl hasn't thought about that much. The other day, when he and a friend were walking down the hall at school and saw a guy with a really bad haircut, Carl blurted out an amazed, "God! Look at that!" When he realized what he'd said, he felt funny at first. But then he figured it was no big deal.

What's the big deal? See Exodus 20:7.

2. Judy is careful not to use God's name in vain. She's careful not to use any of the "really bad" swear words—the kind that give a movie a PG-13 rating. Sure, she says "hell" once in a while when she stubs a toe or breaks a fingernail. She thinks that's pretty mild, considering what she *could* say. And "hell" is just a word, so it's no big deal—right?

What's the big deal? See Matthew 10:28; 12:36.

3. Kevin thinks it's unrealistic to expect a person never to swear. Sometimes you just get so mad at somebody that you've got to use a few "choice words," he says. If he's riding his bike, for instance, and a car practically knocks him into the ditch, he's *got* to say something. And he does—calling the driver an unprintable name or two. Kevin doesn't do this "cussing out" to the person's face, and he does it when nobody else is around to hear. That, he says, makes it no big deal.

What's the big deal? See Matthew 5:22; James 3:9-11; I John 2:9, 10.

4. When Debi and her friends go to the mall, they like to "be themselves." That includes saying pretty much whatever pops into their heads. Often what pops into their heads, and comes out of their mouths, is of the four-letter-word variety. When they sit and talk in one of the mall's fast food places, they sometimes notice older people giving them disgusted looks. Once in a while the older people get up and leave, mumbling things like, "Garbage-mouth kids . . ." But Debi doesn't see what the big deal is. After all, this is how she and her friends talk. Those old people need to get used to it.

What's the big deal? See Ephesians 5:3, 4; Romans 14:13-15, 19.

PROGRAMMING GUIDE

What does Jesus seem to be saying in Matthew 12:33-35 about the link between our hearts and our mouths? _____

_____

Stage 1: Input
Here's where I've been getting most of my input lately (friends, Bible, parents, TV, etc.):

_____

_____

_____

_____

_____

Stage 3: Output
Here's the kind of output I've seen and heard coming from myself lately (words, behavior, expressions, etc.)

_____

_____

_____

_____

_____

_____

Stage 2: Storage
Here's the kind of stuff I've been storing up lately (thoughts, attitudes, feelings, desires, etc.):

_____

_____

_____

_____

_____

_____

Now cross out the source of input that you wrote down under Stage 1 which you think has the worst effect on you. Then circle the source of input that you wrote down under Stage 1 has the most positive effect.

Would you be willing to make an effort in the next couple of weeks to avoid input from the source you crossed out and seek more input from the source that you circled?

Session 15

To teenagers as well as adults, prophecy is one of the most fascinating and confusing subjects of Scripture. Who wouldn't want to know when the world is going to end?

The last century and a half has seen a huge upsurge of interest in the pages of prophecy, especially concerning the "signs of the times." With everything going on in the world today, many question how much longer the planet can survive. With all the wars and warheads, doomsayers and demagogues, terrorists and treaties, is it any wonder that some of your kids may wonder . . .

ARE THESE THE END TIMES?

Specific Aims

• To help kids recognize that, while no one can say for sure when Christ will return, we should live our lives as though He will return at any moment.

Scriptural Support

• Mark 13:32-37
• Luke 21:5-31
• II Peter 3:3-14

Special Preparation

• Bibles
• Copies of Student Sheet 15-A ("Times Check")
• Copies of Student Sheet 15-B ("Vision Test")
• Chalkboard and chalk or newsprint and marker
• Uninflated balloon

1 KILLER SUSPENSE

Bring an uninflated balloon. To start the session, start blowing up the balloon—very slowly. Pause after expelling each breath to heighten the suspense. Walk around the room. Look at your watch. Whistle. Then blow again.

Soon some kids will be holding their ears, anticipating what's going to happen. A few may be screaming by the time the balloon finally bursts.

Discuss:

What were you so uptight about? (We didn't know when the balloon would pop; the uncertainty and suspense of waiting was making everybody tense.)

How could you have lessened the tension you felt? (Run out of the room; grabbed the balloon and popped it.)

Why do you feel relieved now? (We don't have to wait anymore; the big bang is past.)

How would this have been different if you'd known exactly when the balloon would pop? (We could have braced ourselves; we wouldn't have been so nervous.)

A lot of people get tense about a different kind of waiting—waiting for the return of Jesus. They want to know: When is He coming back? Are these the end times? Why do you think they'd want to know?

2 TIMES CHECK

Pass out copies of Student Sheet 15-A ("Times Check") and give kids a chance to read it.

What do you think about this? Do you think this is for real or just a joke?

Give kids a chance to respond. Then comment: **On April 25, 1982, this advertisement ran on a full page of the *New York Times*, the *Los Angeles Times*, the *London Times*, and several other major newspapers across the world.**

Do you think that Christians reading this advertisement thought this was a signal that the end was near? (Probably some did.)

Have kids look up and read Luke 21:5-31 to themselves. Then ask:

What kinds of things does Jesus mention in Luke 21 that will be signs that precede end times?

(Many will come claiming to be "the Christ" [vs. 8];

There will be wars, revolutions, and conflicts [vss. 9, 10];

There will be earthquakes, famines, and pestilences, as well as fearful events and great signs from heaven [vs. 11];

Jesus' followers will be persecuted and have opportunity to be witnesses for Him [vss. 12-15];

Jesus' followers will be betrayed by family and hated by all people [vss. 16, 17];

Jerusalem will be surrounded by armies and trampled by the Gentiles, and the destruction will be great [vss. 20-24];

There will be more signs in heaven and on earth [vss. 25, 26];

Then all will see the Son of Man coming in the clouds with great power and glory [vss. 27, 28].)

Which of the things Jesus mentioned as signs of the end times do you think have already taken place or are taking place?

Expect varied opinions in response to this question and the next. That's fine; there is disagreement among Bible scholars. The point is to help kids make a connection between Jesus' prophetic comments and modern times.

Which do you think have not taken place yet?

Point out that for centuries Christians all over the world have undergone severe persecution for their faith. Many history experts believe that, in this century alone, more Christians have been martyred than ever before in church history.

Point out that some people believe the prophecy concerning Jerusalem being surrounded by Gentile armies was fulfilled in 70 A.D., when the armies of Titus the Roman laid siege to Jerusalem and utterly destroyed it. Not one stone of the temple was left on another (see Luke 21:5-7). Observe, though, that sincere, seeking, believing Christians differ in their understanding of how and when end times prophecies have or have not been fulfilled.

3 LAST DAYS SURVIVAL KIT

Form three teams. **We just read about Jesus saying things like, "Be ready, keep watch, be alert." Your job now, as a team, is to come up with a "Last Days Survival Kit," including everything you think someone would need to be prepared to survive the time described in Luke 21:5-31.**

Once you give teams time to brainstorm their list of essentials, let members of each team tell the larger group some of the things they came up with. You might list these on the board. (Some possibilities: faith, Bible, medicine, food, other believers for support, packed suitcase, telescope [for watching signs in the heavens], etc.)

4 BLIND DATES

Various people have predicted that the end of the world would come on such-and-such a date, only to watch that date come and go without their prediction coming true. Here are some examples:

William Miller, the founder of Adventism, predicted that Christ would return in 1843.

Taze Russell of the Jehovah's Witnesses said Christ would return in 1914.

In 1966, Herbert W. Armstrong and Garner Ted Armstrong of the Worldwide Church of God predicted in 1966 that the kingdom of Christ would come within 10 or 15 years.

Edgar C. Whisenant wrote *88 Reasons Why the Rapture Could Be in 1988.* When the date came and went, he revised the date to January 1989, and then again to September 1989.

Ask: **Any idea why no one's gotten it right yet?**

(We just haven't unlocked the secret formula yet that holds the true date; all the signs haven't been fulfilled yet; all those prophetic passages in the Bible are just symbolic—not to be taken literally, etc.)

Have a volunteer look up Mark 13:32-37 and read it aloud.

Jesus said over and over that we will not know when the end will come. What has Jesus told us to do, rather than trying to figure out when He's coming? (Be ready, alert, and watching.)

5 Don't Give Up

While some people have made the mistake of setting dates for the Lord's return, others have basically given up on the idea that the Lord will return at all.

Have kids turn to II Peter 3:3-14 and read it. Then ask: **Why, according to this passage, has the Lord been so "slow" about coming back?** (He is patient, not wanting anyone to die eternally but everyone to come to repentance [vs. 9].)

What does Peter, the writer of this passage, say about how "the day of the Lord" will come? (It will come like a thief, and with destructive and exposing power [vs. 10].)

What does Peter say ought to be our response? (We ought to live holy and godly lives [vs. 11], making every effort to be spotless and blameless and at peace with Him [vs. 14] as we look forward to and speed His coming [vs. 12].)

If "the day of the Lord" were today, what is one thing you'd wish you'd done differently?

What's one thing you would do exactly the same way?

Let kids think about these questions on their own. Encourage any who are willing to share, but don't require it. Some answers may be quite personal.

Close the session by handing out Student Sheet 15-B ("Vision Test"). Encourage kids to use this as a visual reminder to be alert and ready. They could put it up in a place where they'll see it often—in a locker, for instance. Also urge kids to start working to change the one thing they'd wish they'd done differently if today were "the day."

THE WORLD HAS HAD ENOUGH . . . OF HUNGER, INJUSTICE, WAR.

IN ANSWER TO OUR CALL FOR HELP, AS WORLD TEACHER FOR ALL HUMANITY, THE CHRIST IS NOW HERE.

HOW WILL WE RECOGNIZE HIM?

Look for a modern man concerned with modern problems—political, economic, and social.

Since July, 1977, the Christ has been emerging as a spokesman for a group or community in a well-known modern country. He is not a religious leader, but an educator in the broadest sense of the word—pointing the way out of our present crisis.

We will recognize Him by His extraordinary spiritual potency, the universality of His viewpoint, and His love for all humanity. **He comes not to judge, but to aid and inspire.**

WHO IS THE CHRIST?

Throughout history, humanity's evolution has been guided by a group of enlightened men, the Masters of Wisdom. They have remained largely in the remote desert and mountain places of earth, working mainly through their disciples who live openly in the world. This message of the Christ's reappearance has been given primarily by such a disciple trained for his task for over 20 years.

At the center of this "Spiritual Hierarchy" stands the World Teacher, *Lord Maitreya*, known by Christians as the *Christ*. And as Christians await the Second Coming, so the Jews await the *Messiah*, the Buddhist the fifth *Buddha*, the Muslims the *Imam Mahdi*, and the Hindus await *Krishna*. These are all names for one individual. **His presence in the world guarantees there will be no third World War.**

WHAT IS HE SAYING?

"My task will be to show you how to live together peacefully as brothers. This is simpler than you imagine, my friends, for it requires only the acceptance of sharing."

"How can you be content with the modes within which you now live: when millions starve and die in squalor; when the rich parade their wealth before the poor; when each man is his neighbor's enemy; when no man trusts his brother?"

"Allow me to show you the way forward into a simpler life where no man lacks; where no two days are alike; where the Joy of Brotherhood manifests through all men."

"Take your brother's need as the measure for your action and solve the problems of the world."

WHEN WILL WE SEE HIM?

He has not as yet declared His true status, and His location is known to only a very few disciples. One of these has announced that soon the Christ will acknowledge His identity and **within the next two months** will speak to humanity through a worldwide television and radio broadcast. His message will be heard inwardly, telepathically, by all people in their own language.

From that time, with His help, we will build a new world.

WITHOUT SHARING THERE CAN BE NO JUSTICE;
WITHOUT JUSTICE THERE CAN BE NO PEACE;
WITHOUT PEACE THERE CAN BE NO FUTURE.

—from an advertisement in the *London Times,* April 25, 1982

VISION TEST

E

XP

ECT

ANCY

ALERT

AREYOU

WATCHING

ANDREADY?